FACING THE WORLD

POLITICAL THEOLOGY AND MERCY

Edited by
John K. Downey,
Steve Ostovich, and
Johann M. Vento

Paulist Press
New York / Mahwah, NJ

Cover image by Randi Grace Nilsberg / Alamy Stock Photo
Cover design by Phyllis Campos
Book design by Lynn Else

Library of Congress Catologing-in-Publication Date

Names: Downey, John K., 1948- editor.
Title: Facing the world : political theology and mercy / edited by John K. Downey, Steve Ostovich, and Johann M. Vento.
Description: New York : Paulist Press, 2018.
Identifiers: LCCN 2017021246 (print) | LCCN 2017044586 (ebook) | ISBN 9781587687310 (ebook) | ISBN 9780809153626 (pbk. : alk. paper)
Subjects: LCSH: Mercy. | Political theology. | Metz, Johann Baptist, 1928—Influence. | Catholic Church—Doctrines.
Classification: LCC BV4647.M4 (ebook) | LCC BV4647.M4 F33 2018 (print) | DDC 261.7—dc23
LC record available at https://lccn.loc.gov/2017021246

ISBN 978-0-8091-5362-6 (paperback)
ISBN 978-1-58768-731-0 (e-book)

Published by Paulist Press
997 Macarthur Boulevard
Mahwah, New Jersey 07430

www.paulistpress.com

Printed and bound in the
United States of America

Contents

iii

CONTENTS

Acknowledgments

We begin by thanking the contributors to this volume. The quality of their work is evident in their essays below as it is in all their scholarship. Moreover, on this project, that work was also characterized by a kind of mercy that took the form of their tremendous patience, humor, and goodwill in our collaboration.

We also want to acknowledge the work and support we have received from our colleagues in the New Political Theology Seminar. This is a group of scholars and activists interested in the work of Johann Baptist Metz, some of whom are his former students. We have been meeting biennially at the Research Institute for Philosophy in Hannover under the codirection of Jürgen Manemann and John Downey as we continue to develop ways to collaborate in doing the work of the new political theology.

Our thanks also go to our editor, Christopher Bellitto, and the staff at Paulist Press. Their support and efficiency have been the very condition of possibility for our success in this project.

Two of us also have particular forms of support we want to acknowledge. Johann Vento wishes to thank those with whom she has collaborated in the context of the Mercy Spirituality Program, who have helped to develop her thinking about mercy theology: her students in that program, the Sisters of Mercy, and other colleagues at Georgian Court University and across the wider world of Mercy higher education. She is particularly grateful to Mary Paula Cancienne and Evelyn Saul Quinn for their enthusiasm, creative perseverance, and friendship.

Steve Ostovich would like to thank the Collegeville Institute for Ecumenical and Cultural Research at St. John's University in Minnesota, and especially Donald Ottenhoff, CIECR Director, for making possible his residency in the fall of 2016 as a Killian McDonnell Fellow in Religion and Culture.

Our debts to our families may seem common, but that does not make them any less deep. We owe these loved ones much more for their patience, support, and inspiration than we can adequately acknowledge here.

Finally, we want to thank Prof. Dr. Johann Baptist Metz for his inspiration, creativity, and guidance. This book is dedicated to him in appreciation for his long career as the creator of the new political theology.

PERMISSIONS

Introduction

AN INVITATION

What does it mean for a theology to "face the world"? The new political theology of Johann Baptist Metz is an answer to this question. As Metz puts it, "The new political theology is the attempt to talk about the times, more precisely, to discuss the prevailing historical, social, and cultural situation so that the memory of God found in the biblical traditions might have a future."[1] For Metz this means theology and Christian faith must be mystical and political, that is, our religious experience must engage our concrete social setting.

Like Metz, Pope Francis invites us to face our historical, social, and political situation. And for Francis this becomes an invitation to take up the question of mercy.[2] But we immediately face a problem here. We find ourselves in a world of an ever-increasing gap between the rich and poor, of abject poverty and the use of persons as means to political and economic ends, of denial by authoritarian regimes of political rights and humane living conditions for millions, of the degradation of our physical environment, and of ongoing violence in many forms, including terrorism and the "war on terror," sexual violence, structural racism, mass incarceration, and xenophobia. Here in the United States, we experience growing political and social separation and polarization and the breakdown of civil discourse in facing these issues. The recent Jubilee Year of Mercy pronounced by Pope Francis provided a context for many of us to give voice to our sense that we are living in "dark times" and, as he puts it, amid a "culture of indifference," and challenged us in faith to try to respond to this situation with hope.

This book responds to the Pope's invitation by opening a conversation (actually, several conversations) between the new political

1

theology and the theology of mercy. The contributors to this volume have all been influenced by Metz to some degree. They are asking you to consider mercy from the perspective of political theology; they are helping us to develop a critical imagination for facing the world. Our contributors "face the world" and the many frightening, troubling, and challenging questions we encounter by putting political theology and mercy into dialogue in various ways. We invite you, the reader, to engage in these conversations for yourself, to consider your own place in our world vis-à-vis these and other challenges important to you. We hope that the questions raised by thinking through political theology and mercy together will spark your own deep engagement and creative response as you "face the world."

MERCY AND POLITICAL THEOLOGY

This book does not catalogue every possible meaning of the word *mercy*. Here, we do not engage the long history of the tension between mercy and justice in philosophy and law. Rather, we are in dialogue with the theology of mercy as articulated most clearly, though not exclusively, by Pope Francis in his preaching and teaching, by Walter Kasper in his *Mercy: The Essence of the Gospel and the Key to Christian Life*,[3] and by Jon Sobrino in his earlier foundational work considering mercy from the standpoint of Liberation Theology, *The Principle of Mercy: Taking the Crucified People from the Cross*.[4] This body of work addresses the relation of God's mercy to God's justice, human mercy and justice, the foundational Christian faith in our utter dependence on God's mercy, as well as the dimensions of mercy related to human interaction. Our volume explores this last aspect of mercy, that is, mercy in human interaction, and does so in conversation with the political theology of Johann Baptist Metz.

The categories of his political theology offer the possibility for thinking about mercy critically and practically as a way to respond to our condition. Metz began to formulate his "new political theology" in the years after Vatican II. He conceives of his work as a fundamental theology, that is, a theology concerned with what we're doing when we do theology, with the questions we need to ask, and with what these questions imply about our understanding of ourselves, each other, and our world. Metz operates with an understanding of the world as history characterized by hope in the eschatological promise of God's reign, with an anthropology in which human subjects are essentially political, and with a critical principle of suffering as the universal category for understanding and responding to experience. For the new political theology, faith in God's eschatological promise makes every political structure provisional and subject to criticism as any current order falls short of the political virtues of justice and love.

Metz's theology focuses on remembering the suffering of others as essential.

> Thus this theology works against the constant tendency of all religious worldviews to mythically or metaphysically camouflage the horrific disasters in the world and also works against a speculative retouching and an idealistic smoothing out of the actual course of history in order to finally make victims invisible and their screams inaudible.[5]

For him the early church was a community of narrative and memory centered on Jesus, and Jesus looked first to the suffering of others and not to their sinfulness. An active compassion, seeing the suffering of others and responding somehow, is the fundamental ground and parameter of the Christian perspective. Metz demands we recognize the suffering of the others whom we face and with whom we are called to live in solidarity. And Metz emphasizes that this *memoria passionis*, sensitivity to suffering, this "compassion" as he later calls it, is more a way of living than a concept.

Metz has spoken of a "cultural amnesia" about the history of suffering and of the many ways we first world, "middle class" Christians medicate ourselves against the suffering of the other. He criticizes a northern hemisphere Christianity that is overly privatized, ahistorical, and bourgeois, and that produces a subject compromised in his or her capacity for solidarity with the suffering. Metz engages in a deconstruction of this middle class subject as part of his effort to suggest a new construction of human subjectivity, one that is political, intersubjective, and inclusive of society's victims. He calls for an "anthropological revolution" by which our very sense of ourselves as human subjects is rooted in our solidarity with those who suffer. For the new political theology, faith is a praxis, which means a critically reflective action in

the interest of solidarity with the suffering other. And all this is characteristic of mercy as we understand it.

Much of what has been written about mercy shares the conviction
that mercy, too, is a praxis. The language of mercy speaks of compassion
and solidarity, key terms within the new political theology. Living mercifully would entail the kind of notion of human subjectivity that political theology has characterized as an "anthropological revolution."
This is true of the works referred to earlier. Walter Kasper connects the
Latin *misericordiae* with the German *Barmherzigkeit*, both words for
mercy meaning to have a merciful heart. "In this universal human
sense, *Barmherzigkeit/misericordiae* names an attitude that transcends
one's own egoism and one's own I-centeredness and has its heart not
with itself, but rather with others, especially the poor and the needy of
every kind," and in this self-transcendence it finds "true freedom."[6]

All these insights can be found in Metz's contribution to this volume, the first essay in this book, "1492—Through the Eyes of a European Theologian." Metz here records his response to the experience
of being in South America at the time of the 500th anniversary of the
arrival of Christopher Columbus in the "new world." What strikes him
over and again is the faces of the people he encounters: "Once again,
the faces, and even more the eyes."[7] These are faces of suffering that call
into question the European and Northern culture of domination. And
they call for a new culture, "a new hermeneutical culture…the culture
of recognition of others in their otherness."[8] It is in responding to these
faces, or, in terms of our book's title, in facing the world, that we learn
what mercy is and what it means to "live mercy." And we share Metz's
conviction that such a response is not a matter of pity but a practical
mysticism, a lived response to our call to be bearers of a hope and to live
under an eschatological promise. "In the end, the mysticism Jesus lived
out and taught, which should also have directed the Logos of Christian
theology, is not a narrow mysticism of closed eyes, but an empathetic
mysticism of opened eyes (cf. such as, Luke 10:25–37)."[9]

The authors of the other essays in this volume have all been
inspired by this vision in some way, and we write in conversation with
Metz. Several of us are members of the New Political Theology Seminar that meets in Hannover, Germany. We do not always agree; we
are in conversation. We do not put forth any unified theory of mercy,
but we all explore mercy in light of our conversations with Metz and
each other, and we raise questions about what it might mean to live

4

mercifully. What is the relationship of mercy to compassion? Is the former divine, the latter human? What of forgiveness? What is our hope? Is this hope rational? How do hope and mercy relate to time? What is our hope concretely, that is, can we hope to change our culture of indifference to practices like racism and sexual violence? Where do we find stories of mercy, and where have we met people whose lives might serve to teach us what mercy means? What do we learn from art, from poetry and photographs, to help us respond critically to suffering and in terms of a mercy that is missing in our culture?

THE ESSAYS

The essays that follow provide models for this questioning. We present Metz's "1492" as a cornerstone to the volume, to introduce readers to his unique way of putting theology in dialogue with the reality of the suffering other. In three following sections titled "Incarnation," "Interruption," and "Recognition," we group the essays that explicitly take on, in a variety of ways, the relationship of political theology and mercy.

The two essays in the first section, "Incarnation," each in their own way—through exploring art and history—engage the Christian understanding of incarnation regarding political theology and mercy. They also root us in questions about who we are, what kind of world we find ourselves in, and how mercy speaks to the human condition.

Julia Prinz, VDMF, uses greyscale photography to help us experience mercy in an apocalyptic horizon. This is a matter of hearing the cries of those who suffer to whom we mostly offer only closed ears. She asks us to consider a way of knowing that undermines our practice of rational domination and that is rather a response to what is missing in our awareness of reality. Her photos help us encounter this absence as knowledge, a knowing that demands mercy of us in our living.

John Downey reintroduces us to St. Francis, whose life constituted what Metz might label an anthropological revolution in its openness to suffering and in its giving us a concrete example of merciful living. Downey reminds us of how the life of St. Francis presents a radical model of finding meaning by challenging unjust economic structures. He also encourages us to embrace the spiritual model of Francis for whom mercy is the key to the incarnation that brings solidarity and completes the cosmic hymn.

The three essays under the heading "Interruption" wrestle with understanding time and messianic history in relation to our hope. Michael Kirwan, SJ, helps us see the centrality of time to understanding mercy. Inspired by William Blake's poetic claim that "time is the mercy of eternity," he looks at the importance of time in the thinking of Pope Francis for whom time is prior to space. Kirwan develops an understanding of time using the distinction made by Metz between evolutionary time and messianic time. The latter is key to important political theological concepts like the eschatological proviso and dangerous memories. But Kirwan tempers this with the Pope's insistence that time be understood in terms of the "theology of the people" (of South America), a corrective to any tendencies toward abstraction in liberation theology as well as political theology. In this theology of the people, mercy is a firm but patient hope for political change that guides merciful practice and is supported liturgically and in popular devotion.

Matt Ashley begins by identifying tensions between the thought of Pope Francis and the political theology of Johann Baptist Metz regarding mercy. He then works through these tensions to find what each has to offer as a correction to the other and what we have to learn from both. One difference is that while Pope Francis emphasizes mercy, Metz has written much more about compassion. Pope Francis declares that mercy is divine, compassion is human. Metz distrusts such a distinction if it puts too much emphasis on human sinfulness rather than suffering as the object of merciful activity, but Ashley points out that this distinction resonates with Metz's own rejection of history as self-justifying evolutionary progress in fidelity to the messianic time and reason of God's promise. In the end, what's crucial is understanding mercy as a matter of discipleship and spirituality in what Metz calls the "mystical-political" structure of faith.

Steve Ostovich engages with Metz's understanding of the temporal, interruptive nature of hope and its eschatological horizon. He relates this understanding with Hannah Arendt's thought on natality, a newness that is only possible through forgiveness. He expands this conception to a fuller understanding of mercy and makes the argument that without mercy, hope loses its grounding in reason, and indeed, that mercy is the condition for the very possibility of a hope that gives meaning to action for justice and love.

Finally, the essays in "Recognition" encourage us to see the faces of embodied others as the condition for understanding what it means to live mercifully. Johann Vento starts from her own experience as someone trained in the Green Dot Bystander Intervention Program to challenge us to change our culture of sexual violence. She offers this as a concrete example of the resistance to the prevailing culture of indifference toward suffering called for by Pope Francis as the enactment of mercy. Vento uses Pierre Bourdieu's category of *habitus* as a way to understand and move beyond the difficulty of our overcoming our moral callousness toward sexual violence. This also can give content and direction to our hope: we seek to develop a more merciful *habitus* even as we acknowledge how difficult it is to change our way of being in the world. She puts us on the path to openness to suffering and working for justice that interrupts our indifference and that constitutes what political theologians like Metz and Dorothee Soelle mean by hope.

With John Sheveland we return to *Nostra Aetate* after fifty years, exploring the role of mercy in interreligious dialogue. He engages the political theology of Metz, as well as the comparative theologies of Buddhist teacher John Makranski and Orthodox Rabbi Irving Greenberg, to argue that *Nostra Aetate*'s phrase "rays of truth," present in the world's religions, become evident through interreligious dialogue and relationship as mercy, as "wound healing," redemptive practices in the face of suffering.

Maureen O'Connell notes how shortly before announcing the Jubilee Year of Mercy, Pope Francis publicly referred to Dorothy Day as a "holy American," whose life was a model of faith. O'Connell tells us of significant incidents in Day's story to get at what mercy might mean in the context of race relations. Using a key category of Metz's political theology, O'Connell asks us to see "bourgeois religion" as white religion and challenges us to break out of the "upper room" of whiteness. The result is a shift beyond a concern with racial justice to live lives of racial mercy, acknowledging the costs of an anthropology of domination and seeking forgiveness and change in repentance.

Kevin Burke, SJ, offers a revealing and inspiring reading of the poetry of Denise Levertov. He finds in her work and in her life story a biblically inspired vision of mercy as a way of living in the world, one that echoes many of the concerns of Metz's political theology and that connects resurrection with dangerous memories and mercy in our long walk of faith.

We have described the work of our contributors and the work to which we are inviting you as a conversation about mercy and political theology. As the final essay by Kevin Burke insists, this is a call to risk the dangerous memory of Jesus. On their way to Emmaus, the disciples talk about their fears and hopes. In a sense, we set out to join them. We are not alone in these dark and indifferent times, but we do have to open our eyes. We need to talk about mercy and to face the world. There is always more to say and do. Join us.

NOTES

1. Johann Baptist Metz, "In the Pluralism of Religious and Cultural Worlds: Notes toward a Theological and Political Program," in John K. Downey, ed., *Love's Strategy: The Political Theology of Johann Baptist Metz* (Harrisburg, PA: Trinity Press International, 1999), 167.

2. Pope Francis, *Misericordiae Vultus: Bull of Indiction of the Extraordinary Jubilee of Mercy*, accessed November 13, 2016, https://w2.vatican.va/content/francesco/en/apost_letters/documents/papa-francesco_bolla_20150411_misericordiae-vultus.html.

3. Walter Kasper, *Mercy: The Essence of the Gospel and the Key to Christian Life*, trans. William Madges (New York: Paulist Press, 2014).

4. Jon Sobrino, *The Principle of Mercy: Taking the Crucified People from the Cross* (Maryknoll, NY: Orbis Books, 1994).

5. Johann Baptist Metz, "Facing the World: A Theological and Biographical Inquiry," *Theological Studies* 75, no. 1 (2014): 27.

6. Kasper, *Mercy*, 21–22.

7. Johann Baptist Metz, "1492—Through the Eyes of a European Theologian," this volume, 12.

8. Ibid., 14.

9. Ibid., 15.

1492—Through the Eyes of a European Theologian[*]

Johann Baptist Metz

I

"Come right up to the balustrade," said Bishop Murelli during a liturgy in Caxia. "Come up so that you can see the faces." They were above all, time and again, small faces, black faces, faces that shone—for moments, for a song, for the duration of a cry, a shout. And there were dreams, there were desires in those eyes—or also tears.

Then I saw the other faces, the other eyes: among the *campesinos* eking out the most wretched of existences around the edges of Lima, above all, time and again, among the poor women, and above all— particularly at night—among the street children of São Paulo. I saw the eyes without dreams, the faces without tears, as it were the unhappiness beyond wishing. I saw children's faces, deadened from sniffing a dis- gusting glue as a substitute for opium, the substitute for dreams in a life that is truly forced below the level of dreams, below the limits of tears: poverty that ends up in the wretchedness of being without dreams or tears! Those of whom I am speaking are not sixty or seventy years old, with burnt out, used up dreams; they are three, five years of age, street

* Originally published in the International Theological Review, *Concilium* (1995). ©1995 by *Concilium*. Used with permission.

children with no parents and no one to care for them, and how many of these hundreds of thousands would still be alive if I were to go back?

Finally, I kept seeing the faces of the Indians, faces shaped by the dark shadows of what is called the mysticism of the Andes; in any event, I, the European, would call it a kind of mysticism of mourning. There is constitutional mourning in the Andes. However, among these Indians, faces have long been in the process of modernization. If you spend too long looking at television, your face changes. Will this mourning prove capable of being combined with our Western civilization? Or will we simply develop the Indians out of their mourning? In my view, were that to happen, humankind would be poorer by a hope. I don't want to romanticize. There is nothing romantic about these mourning faces of the Indians, and in any case "romantic" is far too European a category: it is, in fact, a favorite term of disparagement used by those who do not want to concede our own inability to mourn. In my view, these mourning faces are shaped by a distinctive strength, a secret resistance. Against what? Against the hectic acceleration of time, which we have brought about and to which we ourselves have long been subjected? Against the forgetfulness that nests in our modern consciousness? These faces seem to be missing something that we have long forgotten in the name of "progress" and "development." Christian hope is certainly no kind of superficial optimism. The substance of Christian hope is not simply remote from mourning, stripped of any kind of mourning. With the inability to mourn, there ultimately develops an inability to allow oneself to be comforted and to understand or experience any comfort other than mere postponement.

II

Can we Christians here in Europe, can the churches of our country, bear to look at these faces? Can we, do we want to, risk the change of perspective and see our lives as Christians, in the churches—at least for a moment—from the perspective of these faces? Or do we experience and define ourselves exclusively with our backs to such faces? The temptation to do that is great and, unless I am mistaken, it is growing. 1992: who among us did not think primarily of the Single European Market and the new possibilities for trading that had meanwhile opened to it in Central and Eastern Europe? If we in Europe associate 1992 with Columbus, with the quincentenary of his discovery (1492–1992), do we not do so exclusively from our own perspective? Does not a crypto-triumphalism prevent us honestly from adopting any other perspective?

Such questions become more acute when we note the mentality that (in my view) is at present to be found in Europe (and in North America) and is spreading. By way of a definition, I might venture to call it the "everyday postmodernism" of our hearts, which is again putting the so-called Third World at a faceless distance. Is there not at present something akin to a cultural and spiritual strategy of immunizing Europe, a tendency toward a mental isolationism, the cult of a new innocence, an attempt intellectually to avoid the global demands made on us, a new variant of what I once called "tactical provincialism"? What can be described philosophically as postmodern thought—the repudiation of universalist categories, thinking "in differences," in diminished numbers, in colorful fragments—has a parallel in everyday life. Is there not a new mood among us that is again putting the distress and wretchedness of the poor peoples at a greater existential distance from us? Is not a new provincialism spreading among us, a new form of privatization of our lives, the mentality of an onlooker without any obligation to critical perception, a voyeuristic approach to the great situations of crisis and suffering in the world? In our Enlightened European world, are there not increasing indications of a new, as it were, secondary, innocence that is nourished by the impression that while nowadays we are more informed than ever about everything, above all about what threatens us, and about all the crises and terrors in the world, the move from knowledge to action, from information to support, was never so great and so unlikely as it is today? Does not such an impression dispose one to resignation? Or to a flight into myth and its dreams of innocence, remote from action? Is not an overfamiliarity with crises and misery rife among us? In the end, we get used to the crises over poverty in the world that seem increasingly to be a permanent part of the scene, so that we shrug our shoulders and delegate them to an anonymous social evolution that has no subjects.

However, for the church, the sorry reality of these poor lands that cries out to heaven has long been a fateful question, a touchstone of its character as a world church. In the end of the day, the church does not only *have* a Third World church; by now it *is* largely a Third World

11

church, with an indispensable history of European origins. In view of the mass misery that cries out to heaven (or no longer cries out because its language and dreams have long been shattered), the church cannot reassure itself that here it is experiencing the tragedies of a time shift in a world that is coming together with increasing rapidity. Nor can it tell itself that these poor are the victims or even the hostages or their own heartless oligarchies. The world church needs to spell out and take seriously what was said biblically in the language of an archaic itinerant Christianity preached around the villages: "What you did to the least...." The European church may not, therefore, as it were, in a postmodern way, allow its criteria to be talked out or belittled under the pressure of circumstances and mentalities. It may not withdraw from the tension between mysticism and politics into a thinking in terms of myths that is remote from history. In the end, with its creed "suffered under Pontius Pilate," it is and remains attached to concrete history, to that history in which there is crucifixion, torture, suffering, hatred, weeping—and loving. No myth can give it back that innocence it loses in such a history.

Certainly, the church is not primarily a moral institution, but the bearer of a hope. Its theology is not primarily an ethic but an eschatology. But the roots of its power lie precisely in the helplessness of not giving up the criteria of responsibility and solidarity and leaving the preferential option to the poor only to the poor churches. All this has to do with the greatness and the burden that is laid on us with the biblical word *God*. It does not remove us from social and political life, but simply takes away the basis of hatred and violence from this life. It calls on all men and women to walk upright, so that all can kneel voluntarily and give thanks with gladness.

III

Once again, the faces, and even more the eyes. With what eyes was Latin America, was this "Catholic continent," discovered? At the beginning of the times we in Europe call *modern*, at the beginning of the modern period, an anthropology of domination was developing— secretly, and overlaid by many religious and cultural symbols. Man understood himself increasingly as a dominant subject, there to put nature under his control. His identity was formed by this lordly sub-jection, this seizing of power over nature. His eyes looked downward. His logic became a logic of domination, not of recognition: a logic of assimilation and not of otherness. All virtues that did not contrib-ute to domination—friendliness and gratitude, a capacity for suffering and sympathy, mourning and tenderness—faded into the background, were cognitively depotentiated, or entrusted to the world of women in a treacherous "division of labor." We may have long failed to notice the features of this anthropology and logic of domination because the pressure toward subjection very soon shifted outward—against alien minorities, alien races, alien cultures. Obviously, the history of Euro-pean colonization has its roots here. Who would venture to dispute that this mechanism of domination continually made its way through into the history of Christian mission as well?

Certainly, the project of European modernity contributed, and continues to contribute, quite different features. Thus, within it—in the processes of political Enlightenment—there developed a reason that seeks to be practical in achieving freedom and justice. For a long time, it was encoded in European terms. So what came about in the meanwhile was a developing *secular* Europeanization of the world—by way of science, technology, and economics; in short, by way of the world domination of Western rationality. However, this caught up the whole world in a tremendous frenzy of acceleration. The dawn of the indus-trial age already brought with it great impoverishment and misery in Europe, especially in the last century. Although the pace of the Euro-pean industrial development has been quite rapid, and Europe has changed more in the last 150 years than in the whole of the past 2,000, among us, the development, nevertheless, took place in slow motion as compared with the pace of the process of industrialization that can be noted, for example, in Brazil. The growing acceleration of this modernization, this industrial and technical development—above all, in post-urban metropolises such as São Paulo—seems to be matched by an increase in impoverishment that has grown exponentially. The development has no time to develop. It destroys the time of human beings, who seem to be crushed between premodern conditions of life and rule and postmodern technology.

The political culture that seeks freedom and justice for all can be established only if among us and in those Latin American countries it is combined with another culture that, for want of a better term, I might call a new hermeneutical culture: the culture of the recognition of others in their otherness, with the way in which they form a social and cultural identity, with their own images of hope and recollection. It is imperative that supposedly neutral economic and technological forces that are allegedly free of political and moral pressures should be tested by them. Only such a culture of recognition makes possible a respectable and redemptive interchange between Europe and these countries. Indeed, in the end, the European spirit itself is endangered by the process of modernization that it set in motion: it increasingly acts as an automatic process, and increasingly, human beings in these processes are merely their own experiments, and less and less their memories.

IV

From the very beginning, with its consciousness of mission, Christianity struggled for a culture of the recognition of the other. What was to be normative for this consciousness of mission was not Hellenistic thinking in terms of identity and assimilation, but the biblical notion of the covenant, according to which, like is not known by like, rather, unlikes know one another by recognizing one another. One example of this is the dispute between Peter and Paul along with the dispute at the Apostolic Council over the question of whether gentile Christians were to be circumcised. This recognition of the others in their otherness is expressed in the refusal of the Jewish Christian Paul to subject the gentile Christians to circumcision. So, at the roots of the biblical tradition lie the impulses to a new hermeneutical culture: any "will to power" is really alien to it, in the recognition of the others in their otherness. This hermeneutical culture was again obscured in the history of Europe; it also faded into the background in the history of the church. So, with what eyes was the Latin American continent "discovered"? Did this early Christian hermeneutic of recognition play a normative role? Or was the process of Christianization of America not far more (if not exclusively) accompanied by a questionable hermeneutic of assimilation, a hermeneutic of domination, that had no eyes for the trace of God in the otherness of the others and that, therefore, continually also violated the culture of these others it did not understand, and

14

made them victims? At any rate, we must use this question to measure all the ceremonial words spoken on the occasion of the quincentenary.

V

The church does not hope for itself. Therefore, it does not need to split its own history — in a suspiciously ideological fashion — in order only to display the sunny side of this history, as those must do who "have no hope." To concede failure does not mean falling into a neurotically arrogant cult of self-accusation. It is quite simply a matter of honoring our eschatological hope and venturing conversion and new ways in the light of it.

That also applies, *mutatis mutandis*, to our Christian theology. I have often asked myself why so little attention is paid to the history of human suffering. Is that the sign of a particularly strong faith? Or is it perhaps just the expression of a historical way of thinking, detached from any situation and empty of humanity, a kind of idealism equipped with a high degree of apathy in the face of the catastrophes and downfalls of others? The new political theology in Europe developed, among other things, out of the attempt to make the cry of the victims of Auschwitz unforgettable in the *logos* of theology. And the theological impetus of liberation theology, as I understand it, comes from the attempt to make it possible to hear the cry of the poor in the *logos* of theology and make the face of strange other men and women recognizable in it; that is, to interrupt the flood of ideas and the closed character of systematic argumentation with this cry and with these faces. That may make the language of theology small, poor, and completely unsolemn. But if it becomes that, it will come close to its original task. In the end, the mysticism Jesus lived out and taught, which should also have directed the *logos* of Christian theology, is not a narrow mysticism of closed eyes, but an empathetic mysticism of opened eyes (cf. Luke 10:25–37). The God of Jesus cannot be found either here or there if we ignore its perceptions.

I

INCARNATION

1

Mercy through the Luminesce of Greyscale

Photographic Images and the Political Theology of Johann Baptist Metz[*]

Julia D. E. Prinz, VDMF

> *To see is to see into.*
>
> —Ansel Adams

THE RELATIONSHIP MANAGER

Recently I received a call from my bank. Instead of hearing a cue for an "assistant" or for "customer service," the automated voice advised me that a "relationship manager" would be with me shortly. I wondered about this new way of framing the assistance one needs to resolve issues with one's bank account. What were the bank's marketing officers thinking? What meaning did they give to *relationship*, especially if they planned to "manage" mine?

---

[*] Photographs in this essay are the property of the author and are used by permission.

How is language used here? Does it imply that the imperatives of commerce and financial exchange would come to define—and manage—human relationships? The terminology used by the company, probably following some new marketing rules, illuminated for me the depth of the manipulation of language. The World Wars of the twenty-first century might not only erupt as armed conflicts between distinguishable nations, but also, the attacks might be launched by manipulative, demagogical, and calculative language against the language of human authenticity, vulnerability, and intimacy. The language that is used feeds into the imagination of control and possession, also found in fundamentalism, against the imagination of human dignity and freedom; it fuels the imperatives of resource domination against the imperatives of human hunger.

What might it mean, in the context of this reality of loss of language, to ponder mercy? Might mercy be an act of imagination against the escalation of violence, the displacement of peoples, and the destruction of ancient civilizations all over the world? Might mercy hold the capacity of resistance on behalf of messy, unmanageable human relationships and a messy but human world, and against a world contrived from the dominance of a vast expanding economic globalization and the concomitant concentration of global resources and wealth in the hands of a few?

To begin addressing these questions, this essay explores the nuance of mercy that entails resistance. I develop the theological discussion in dialogue with forms of black-and-white photography to illustrate how they have a distinctive capacity to embody our understandings. Johann Baptist Metz builds a unique bridge between what I call the two art forms of theology and photography through his use of language in his political theology.[1] The language of Metz, by which he reflects on the Christian mystery, structures my discourse on mercy in dialogue with the visual art of photography. I am using three different aspects of Metz's theology in my argument: mercy as a "knowing born in missing" (*Vermissungswissen*), mercy as a cry (*Schreiwort*), and mercy as an apocalyptic horizon that insists on more than merely "being good." In the concluding section of this essay, I link these interlocking aspects of mercy around the theme of incarnation, especially as this emerges in Metz's provocative essay "Caro Cardo Salutis."[2] The importance of the incarnation does not only impose itself on this discourse because of the reality of mercy and Pope Francis's direction of declaring a Year of Mercy, but also because of the dialogue partner of photography. Art, in its relationship to the mystery of the incarnation, is at the core of a Christian understanding of art per se. As Rahner writes, "If theology is not identified *a priori* with verbal theology, but is understood as a person's total self-expression in so far that this is born in God's self-communication, then religious phenomena in the arts are in themselves a moment within theology taken in its totality."[3]

The photograph that serves as the visual introduction into the essay gives its own interpretation of Rahner's and Metz's reflection on the incarnation (see plate 1). The hand in the photograph holds the door of a small battered truck without ventilation or windows transporting twelve men and women through scorching heat to their construction worksite in the Philippines. It is through this hand that we see into the dark of that truck at every stoplight. It is that hand that speaks of "Caro Cardo Salutis." Precisely by veiling what we see, it cries out in the flesh.

Interruption (plate 1)

A MERCY OF RESISTANCE

When Pope Francis stepped outside of the standard cycle of ecclesiastical order and declared a Year of Mercy, he opened the door of mercy, literally and figuratively, to our human world. The open door invites us to imagine a different way of relating to one another. It bids us to peer behind doors held shut by desperate hands and perceive there the human suffering hidden within (see plate 1). In an unusual fashion, after only three years in office, the pontiff inaugurated a symbolic shift in ecclesial focus, language, and rhetoric. He made a powerful move in declaring the Year of Mercy, adding yet another visual and linguistic icon to the humanizing preaching and praxis that shaped his ministry from the first day he assumed the office of the Bishop of Rome. Francis shifted the ecclesial attention away from the centrality of judgment and away from the setting up of immutable boundaries around Catholic moral and liturgical practice. He has been focused on the shared life among all human beings, independent of their beliefs, but rather governed by attention to the most vulnerable, marginalized, and suffering individuals, groups, and societies. The pope opened the impermeable exclusive circles of Roman Catholic self-understanding to an invitation for mutual support, solidarity, and tolerance.

However, mercy is a far more unkempt concept than it might seem at first sight, and it is not always clear that its grey tones are fully appreciated. It is instructive to survey the images of mercy autoselected by a casual, postmodern Google search of the word *mercy*. Pages after virtual pages of colorful, harmonious, tension-free images pop up: images often buffered by soft filters, images nearly always conveyed in a romantic idiom, images that print best with a high-gloss finish, images that leave nearly no room for grey tones, uncertainties, or painful absence. The *sine qua non* in the globalizing, controlled image of mercy is clear: mercy implies an idealized impression of nature and of human relationships. In the world of relationship managers and maximized global economic profit, one could feel as if mercy fits into that polished worldview. It defines a religious imperative to manage human relationships out of an illusionary nostalgia.[4] It is alluring to look at but impossible to live.

Do we need to rescue our images of mercy from the hands of relationship managers if we want to take Pope Francis's invitation seriously? Could it be that our use of *mercy*, if we are not careful, will aggravate the circumstances of a world that is ripping apart at its seams, instead of lifting it up?

From a photographic point of view, there is more to the difference between the glossy color photography described above and black-and-white photography than perhaps directly meets the senses. Black-and-white photography, by way of counterimages in greyscales, challenges the showy, garish, glossy, romantic images and the "final management" of relationship and mercy.[5] Artistic black-and-white photography has the capacity to question the idealizing reproduction of color expressions that flood the everyday world of commercials and that turn even religious images into propaganda. Part of the suggestive power in nearly propagandistic color images is the lack of ambiguity and artistic contrast. Much more than color photography, black-and-white photography receives its character by way of perceiving contrasts: granite against sand, the sharp edge and the endless horizon, the cliff above the stretching, shimmering water, "the brink" before "the elusive deep horizon" (see plate 2).[6] Its power lies precisely in its absence of color. Its connotations arise from missing the density of color. Even the "grain" of a black-and-white photograph reminds one of the art of unpolished clarity paying homage to a reality that exists in grey zones (see plate 3).[7]

All photography, but again, especially black-and-white photography, focuses on some specific object in relation to its horizon. However, the nature of that focus can vary. For example, the individual element might be brought forward through its relationship with the whole, as when one perceives a solitary tree on a rock caught between seashore and clouded sky. However, the focus might fall upon entire areas within the photograph, such as different grades of light bands and bends in a cliff high above light-reflecting water (see plate 2). Furthermore, adding grain to the light bands while increasing the image noise veils certain areas of the image and brings forward a shifted point of focus, like a mysterious waterfall, its source unknown (see plate 3).[8]

The Solitary Shore (plate 2)

The Source (plate 3)

SHADOWS AND SHADES OF GREY

The essence of artistic black-and-white nature photography is to hold *what is missing*—the missing light, the missing perfection—*in* the translucence of fog, mist, rain, dirt, and even smudge. It is this kind of black-and-white photography that questions the images of mercy distributed by popular piety and Google search alike. In the remaining sections of this essay, I focus especially on black-and-white nature or outdoor photography, photographs that attempt to capture a whole scene. Excellent examples abound in the works of Alfred Stieglitz, Ansel Adams, and Mary Randlett.[9] I do not attend to such black-and-white genres as *studio photography*, *portrait photography*, or synthetic *macro photography*.[10]

What image of mercy can be perceived in such monochrome greyscale tradition of nature photography? Rather than the specific image of a given thing or scenery, I suggest a greyscale image of absence, doubt, desire, and of what is missing—corresponding with images of fog, rain, and mist. Those natural elements reveal by the way of veiling the perfect image. They reveal what individuals experience through the picture rather than in the picture (see plate 4).

Descending (plate 4)

This kind of black-and-white nature photography of veiling and missing, of greyscale and absence, corresponds to theological questions regarding mercy. It is a description of mercy that is characterized by vulnerability, scars, absence, and the knowledge of what is missing. One of the architects of contemporary political theology, Johann Baptist Metz, developed the category of *Vermissungswissen*, "missing as a form of knowing" or, as I often translate it, "a knowing absence," in contrast to the glorifying victory song of a Christian mythos that saturates all suffering in the juice of a final Hallelujah mercy.[11] In my opinion, Metz's incisive understanding of *Vermissungswissen* serves as a theological key capable of unlocking a spirituality nascent in black-and-white photography. This in turn provides important images for the horizon of mercy that Francis seeks to claim as a signpost for Christian life in the world today. Metz introduces the concept of *Vermissungswissen* into the theological discourse to provide philosophical resistance to the contemporary theological tendency to rely on Kant's "pure reason" as the defining feature of the human being. It correlates with his insistence on memory in anamnestic reason.

> For anamnestic reason, being attentive to God means hearing the silence of those who have disappeared. It does not relegate everything that has vanished to existential insignificance. Knowing remains at root a form of missing [*Vermissungswissen*], without which not only faith but the human him or herself would disappear. Such memorative knowing, which is always on the lookout for the forgetfulness of the forgotten…would really be the organon of a theology that tries to confront our most highly progressive and developed consciousness with the cries and accusations of that past which is systematically forgotten in it. It would allow the outlines of a landscape of theodicy to become recognizable, even in our world.[12]

For Metz, "missing" constitutes a primer of knowledge. He would ask epistemologically: What comes first, missing or knowing? How will you know without missing? This resonates with the way of knowing and perceiving developed by black-and-white photographers who practice *contemplative photography*.[13] I am using the term *contemplative photography* in this context not only as the technical term minted by Karr and Wood, along with the Miksang Institute, but also in a more general way. Traces of important contemplative dimensions appear in some of the photographers who, by focusing on what is missing, have most influenced my understanding of photography. The award-winning

Brazilian photographer Sebastião Salgado explains in his autobiography what silence, brokenness, and awareness have to do with seeing what is missing: "Without patience you cannot be a photographer."[14] This is not simply a technical exhortation, but rather an attitude of life or faith. Similarly, American photographer Beth Moon focuses on the most ancient trees of the world to make memory of thousands of years of lost history.[15] Gerry Sharp, an unusual but beloved student of Ansel Adams, attended to a "sense of human absence above all" in her photography, as her biographer, Gretchen Gardner, points out.[16] Finally, Paul Caponigro, another important contemporary American photographer, expresses well a broad understanding of contemplative photography:

> I believe the process [of taking a photograph] should involve not just the chemical but also the alchemical, linking the photographic tradition to the greater tradition of calling forth a higher consciousness. In the end, toll and materials must allow access to the inner realm of awareness, which also is capable of transcending preconceptions....Recording the light of the outer subject can be linked with gaining access to one's inner light.[17]

All photography is about seeing, but this is especially the case with contemplative photography, the photography that understands itself as a spiritual contemplative praxis. It takes the following as its central question: What are you missing in your experience of your surroundings? We cannot engage this question simply by taking a snapshot or a selfie in some once-in-a-lifetime setting, even if the outcome is a marvelous picture. Contemplative photography "learns to see what is missing" in the perceptions of the situation. It follows that intuition until it learns how to see and act.

For photographers who align themselves with the school of contemplative photography, the waiting and perception of what is missing in the situation at hand is crucial. Even though, of course, all photography undergoes a search for a focus, contemplative photography does not primarily ask, "What is there?" Rather, its questions probe *what is not there? what is absent?* The "knowledge" shared by the contemplative black-and-white photographic image emerges from its open eyes in silence: what is missing points to what will become the focus of the image. Something similar appears in Ansel Adams's photographic theory. His reflections shed light on the field of contemplative photography, for he refuses to call his black-and-white photographs "abstract." Instead, he sees in them what he calls an "extract." I suspect this has something to do with his spirituality of black-and-white photography. The central aim of his process of extraction is to realize what is missing in the picture, whether light, objects, or human beings. The elimination and concentration process does not have abstraction as a goal but rather the extraction of the whole as seen in a single specific composition, a simple shadow line across a snowfield, for example.[18]

MERCY AS *SCHREIWORT*

Pope Francis's call for a Year of Mercy sheds light on this theologically relevant shift of perception exemplified by the practice of contemplative photography. His iconic *opening of the door* to the Year of Mercy is endangered by a speculative and theoretical knowledge that pays no attention to what is missing, that gives no weight to human questions and challenges, but instead depends entirely on preformulated religious affirmations, instructions, and ethical demands. Isn't it easy to forget the cry that lies in mercy? Doesn't the need for mercy emerge from brokenness and loss? And is Christian mercy truly a blanket covering it all? Or isn't every act of mercy always the act of claiming God in God's final mercy, beyond all human imagination? Perhaps the power of the invitation in a life of mercy is not just fulfilled by the important acts of mercy, but moreover in the cry for mercy, the insistence of mercy even in the experience of its human incompleteness while finally missing God's all-embracing mercy integrated with God's justice. Perhaps the crying out to God is the only way we can make present what is absent—God's mercy and justice.[19]

The Year of Mercy is not simply the declaration of a reality of faith that demands certain ethical behaviors, but is rather the outcry to the heavens—and God in them—for mercy in this world. One could say it is an understanding of mercy that is more deeply rooted in the lament tradition than in the resurrection narratives. It invites us, in a Year of Mercy, to understand how mercy is a *Schreiwort*, a scream. The scream for mercy penetrates the terrible suffering of the world. It enters the dark, it embraces what is unclear and full of doubt. It imagines the fog and names the destruction. In this instance, mercy is not a reality to be demanded and it is not a "truth of faith" to be interpreted by an ecclesiastical relationship manager with indulgences. Mercy is the only petition, the only scream *unto* God[20] that will never end as long as humanity exists in its limited and broken relationships.

Returning to photography, it is important to ask how one might express mercy as a *Schreiwort*. Instead of relying on affirmative statements of mercy given in optimistic color photographs, the point of departure would entail the ambiguous possibilities afforded by black-and-white photography. How would a photographic journey pay homage to this shift from the romanticism of color images (with their immediate visual impact and preformulated ideological and religious understandings) to *Vermissungswissen*, the knowing absence, of monochrome shades of grey (characterized by searching, lamenting, and missing)? (See plate 5.)

Pitched at the Brink (plate 5)

The proclamation of the Year of Mercy by Pope Francis is not only important, in my opinion, because it calls people out of their narrow judgments, but especially because it draws attention to the abhorrent violence and injustice in this world. We need to bring what is missing—peace and justice—unto God. Whether we do so by screaming, wailing, or embracing deep silence, it is the invitation to never give up longingly calling on God's mercy. This does not represent a cover-up or an attempt to manage despair. Rather, it entails the profound *metanoia* from a world thrown onto itself to a world thrown unto

God. Mercy as *Schreiwort* breaks open the technocratic management of society with the soaring tones of the longing for mercy. At the same time, it brings the margins into focus. Mercy as *Schreiwort*—born out of a *Vermissungswissen* that is, in turn, rooted in the lament Psalms and *mashal* traditions of the Scriptures—reveals the complexity of the reality of faith that we describe with Pope Francis's appeal.

MERCY VERSUS "BEING GOOD"

One well-known parable (*mashal*) that frequently appears as an image of mercy in the Year of Mercy comes from Matthew 20:1–16. We know the scene well: a group of day laborers who are waiting for work are sent to work in the vineyard at different hours of the day. At the end of the day, the vineyard owner (who declares himself to be good) gives *all* the day laborers the same pay, although clearly some of them have worked the whole day and others only an hour. This causes unrest among the workers, but the last words of the owner attempt to quiet their complaints: "Am I not allowed to do what I choose with what belongs to me? Or are you envious because I am generous?" (Matt 20:15).

Traditional interpretations of this and other parables like it seek to draw a direct analogy between the vineyard owner and God. As such, the moral of the story in this view focuses on how God's judgment turns our judgments upside down. This reversal of judgments is seen to exemplify mercy par excellence. I choose this parable because it seems such a perfect image of mercy, but with the help of William Herzog and Luise Schottroff,[21] one can begin to understand that this parable is far more complex than our usual interpretations allow. This complexity comes to light when our focus on mercy in the interpretation of this text begins to reflect some of the grey tones and unclarity around the victorious end statement of the vineyard owner. Focusing on the day laborers provokes new questions. How far can they stretch a single denarius? Who is missing in the scene that the denarius needs to feed? What are the social dynamics exercising invisible control over these relationships?

Herzog and Schottroff develop a sophisticated argument for which I can only provide a sketch in two points. First, the situation of day laborers in the ancient world was one of absolute desolation. They were worth even less than slaves, for slaves at least represented an asset in which the owner had a vested interest. Day laborers generally were asked to do the hardest work. If they were injured or killed on the job, the owner would incur no loss. And for all that, they never received a wage sufficient to feed their families: one denarius for a day's work represented the lowest end of a wage scale. A single person might survive on that, but not an entire family. It is interesting to further note that the day labor of the women and children of the family receives no mention at all: if the day laborer lives on the lowest rung of the socioeconomic ladder, the women and children must have worked in even worse conditions to make ends meet. Finally, day laborers would be hired only for the hours they were needed, so a market imperative required that the labor managers (the ancient world's relationship managers) go out three or more times a day to hire additional workers. In that way, while the workers have too little work, the manager cuts his expenses by hiring only for the hours that he needs to complete the day's tasks.[22]

Second, the vineyard owner is presented as a small Roman landowner with the full property right guaranteed and supported by Roman law. This Roman landowner's self-description insists that he is good (*agathos*). Interestingly, up to this point, the parable would assume that only God can be described as good (*agathos*) (see, e.g., Mark 10:18; Matt 19:17–19). No human being could earn this description, so after the Roman landowner describes himself as good, we encounter a suggestive eschatological remark in the verse following the parable: "The last will be first, and the first will be last" (Matt 20:16). The parable mines Jewish memory, as Matthew does in various other places: the ones who own no land are always seen as the last or the lost. Not surprisingly, many prayers directed at the reversal of such fortunes do so by proclaiming the eschatological hope where these people, above all, enjoy the fruit of their own lands (see, e.g., Matt 5:5; Ps 37:11).

The questions raised and the analysis provided by Herzog and Schottroff are thought provoking. Is the Roman landowner as good as God? Or might it be that his action, although perhaps seen as good, does not correspond to the divine "goodness"—that is, the expression of justice and mercy—that a Jewish believer would attribute to God? Could one even understand that this landowner—who blames the victims for envying his Roman property rights and giving them not enough money to even sustain their families—stands for a counterimage to

God? Or at least a very incomplete image of God that only shows how different and far more substantial the kingdom of God should be? The parable does not end with day laborers reconciled. It seems to lay the groundwork for further protest.

It is not necessary to canonize any one interpretation of this parable to recognize that the cautions recommended by Herzog and Schottroff against a tendency to equate the Roman landowner's generosity with God's mercy are of crucial importance in discussing the invitation to live the Year of Mercy. In line with their intuitions, an apocalyptic horizon rips across the landscape of Pope Francis's invitation to mercy.[23] Mercy is not an endpoint we have reached. Mercy is an apocalyptic reality of God toward which we are living. Without this apocalyptic dimension, mercy again devolves into the managing of relationships by a Roman landowner.

Returning to the photographic visual reflections, one is reminded by this discussion of apocalyptic horizons of the conscious artistic choice to let part of the image grow beyond its frame (see plate 6). This technique, already utilized in medieval art to show the "extra" or "subaltern meaning" of the artistic representation, is well established in photography and, again, especially practiced in black-and-white photography. The part that lies "beyond the frame" is the part that the audience will miss; they will wonder about, ask after, and perhaps even long for the full picture, the whole image. But perhaps, as with the understanding of mercy, the human limits will mostly meet with the reality that there never is a "full picture" until the end of time.

Filaments (plate 6)

CARO CARDO SALUTIS

The vision of contemplative photography, with its insight into the invitation of a Year of Mercy, and further illuminated by Metz's theological epistemology of *Vermissungswissen*, corresponds to the central role of the incarnation in Christian faith. As the ancient belief confesses, "Salvation lies in the flesh" (*Caro cardo salutis*). This confession of the early church speaks directly against every tendency to spiritualize the discourse on mercy. The ever-present threat of gnostic interpretations, from the earliest church to the present day, makes it appear that mercy involves a spiritual process that is independent of or at least superior to the fleshly corporal experience. In this context, Metz writes, "The human being is not on one hand soul and on the other hand flesh, but rather truly one is the reality of the other. The reality of one's flesh, is not distinct from the real soul, in as far as this soul only can be real, in her self-expression bound by time and space."[24] If the body is the expression of the soul in such way that it is not limiting, but rather creates the reality from the body, how do we conceive mercy? We distinguish acts of mercy from the soul perceiving mercy, but this leaves open the question of whether mercy is at all possible without the terrestrial, earthbound, fleshy existence of the soul.

If the incarnation is the compass needle for understanding mercy, Metz urges us to "think in the simplest of all experiences that we often would describe as only bodily: to laugh, to cry, like in the tears of Sara, in hunger, in thirst, or in bending oneself over the cisterns in the desert…it is here where fullness of life unfolds; it is not something one can simply renounce. Heaven and Earth have met and they love each other in such a human sensibility, in such a simple gesture."[25] It is the embodiment of the absence that provides another dimension for the understanding and perception of mercy.

This unique and even ambiguous connection between absence and embodiment leads Metz to the emphasis that he formulates regarding anamnestic reason: remembering the suffering of the other.[26] Such remembering imbues theology and spirituality with an interest in history, not in categories, and in epistemological experience, not in ontological apprehension. Speaking of his political theology, Metz insists,

The category of memory plays a central role; my work does not want to let go of the apocalyptic metaphors of the history of faith, and it mistrusts an idealistically smoothed out eschatology. Above all, the whole of my theological work is attuned by a specific sensitivity for theodicy, the question of God in the face of the history of suffering in the world, in "his" world....Whoever talks about God in Jesus' sense will always take into account the way one's once pre-formulated certainties are wounded by the misfortune of others.[27]

That is the reason Metz asks, Are such a faith—a faith that dares history—and such a mysticism—a mysticism that opens its eyes to the suffering of others—consoling?[28] Monochrome photographs, with their special sensitivity to absence, provoke in me similarly disturbing questions. Are they easy? Are they smooth? Do they console? (See plate 7.)

Resisting Demolition (plate 7)

In Metz, then, we encounter a contemporary Catholic theologian who, through his emphasis on historicity, makes memory, language, and the limitation of human perception the central points of theological discourse. Consequently, mercy is not limited to affirmative dogmatic formulations but rather unfolds in the vulnerable questions of a longing absence. Those vulnerable questions could perhaps be called the vertebrae of monochrome photography. In its inherent melancholy, black-and-white photography voices such longing absence in rather silent ways in contrast to the affirmative dogmatics of color (see plate 8).

Reminiscence (plate 8)

Mercy as *Schreiwort*, mercy born in *Vermissungswissen*, mercy as an apocalyptic horizon—all three of these descriptions widen the invitation of Pope Francis, which too easily can be understood as a limited ethical demand, a Christian "solve all" blanket or a "feel good" invitation. All three ways of broadening the concept of mercy are anchored in a political theology and mirrored in an engagement with greyscale monochrome photography. Such photography and political theology enter together into fruitful dialogue where ambiguity and questions of human existence become more important than clarity and victory. Like political theology, black-and-white photography springs from the earth. Salvation and the life of grace occur in the flesh. As Metz notes, "In this body our final image has been unfolded; and the earth herself is so much a part of our being that without her we ourselves would never be able to understand or love."[29]

NOTES

1. In the definition of theology as art, I am inspired by a quotation from Brother Thomas, an award-winning and well-known U.S. ceramic artist, who said, "I am not doing art, I am doing theology." In *Pucker Gallery Catalogue: Continued Beginning—Tenmoku Master Works by Brother Thomas* (Boston: Pucker Gallery, 2009), 16.

2. This largely unknown early writing of Metz, which is one of his most brilliant essays, has finally been republished in volume 2 of his collected works. "Caro Cardo Salutis—Zum Christlichen Verstaendnis des Leibes (1962)," *Fruehe Schriften, Entwuerfe und Begriffe, Gesammelte Schriften*, Band 2, ed. J. Reikerstorfer, trans. J. D. E. Prinz (Freiburg: Herder, 2015), 166–79.

3. Karl Rahner, "Art as *Locus Theologicus*," in Gesa Elsbeth Thiessen, *Theological Aesthetics: A Reader* (London: SCM, 2004), 219.

4. A striking similarity appears between this contrast—the mercy of the relationship manager and the mercy of Pope Francis—and the contrast Metz makes between memory as nostalgia and dangerous memory; see Johann Baptist Metz, *Faith in History and Society: Toward a Practical Fundamental Theology*, trans. J. Matthew Ashley (New York: Crossroad Publishing, 2007), 105–6.

5. It seems no coincidence that Roland Barthes wrote his classic *Camera Lucida: Reflections on Photography* while he was in grief about the death of his mother. Significantly, he places a black-and-white photograph of his mother at the center of the second part of the book. Barthes's reflections are precisely sparked by the absence and presence of his mother in the photography, by the ambiguity the image is transmitting. *Camera Lucida: Reflections on Photography*, trans. Richard Howard (New York: Hill and Wang, 1981).

6. The quoted phrase is taken from Denise Levertov's inspiring poem "The Blind Man's House at the Edge of the Cliff," in *A Door in the Hive* (New York: New Horizons, 1989), 10. I am grateful to Don Gelpi, Kevin Burke, Mark Bosco, and Melissa Bradshaw for leading me to connect my work on photography with the political poetry of Denise Levertov. See Bruce Barnbaum, "Color," in *The Art of Photography* (Santa Barbara, CA: Rocky Nook, 2010), 81–83.

7. Regarding these general comments on black-and-white photography, see Ansel Adams, *Examples: The Making of 40 Photographs*

(New York: Little, Brown and Co., 1983). Regarding texture, see his discussion of the photo titled "Sand Dunes," 149.

8. For further background on the photographic theory followed here, see White Minor, *Zone System Manual: Previsualization, Exposure, Development, Printing; The Ansel Adams Zone System as a Basis of Intuitive Photography* (Hastings-on-Hudson, NY: Morgan & Morgan, 1968).

9. See, e.g., Alfred Stieglitz, *Camera Work: A Photographic Quarterly* (New York: Stieglitz, 1903–1917); Ansel Adams, *Classic Images*, with James Alinder and John Szarkowski (Boston: Little, Brown and Co., 1986); Mary Randlett, *Landscapes* (Seattle: University of Washington Press, 2007).

10. Giving adequate attention to these latter genres lies beyond the limits of this chapter. However, it should be noted that some professional-commercial black-and-white photography, especially in its low grain, precise representation of the object, suffers the same fate as the idealized representation of color photography, despite the obvious difference between these basic photographic forms. Professional photography achieves its commercial success along with what I ironically nickname the *Appleization* of photography in the apotheosis of catchy photographs on giant billboards. The "snapshot" as art leads to banality for both.

11. Johann Baptist Metz, "Exkurs: Vermissungswissen Theologisch," in *Memoria Passionis: Ein Provozierendes Gedächtnis in Pluralistischer Gesellschaft* (Freiburg im Breisgau [u.a.]: Herder, 2011), 28–34.

12. Johann Baptist Metz, "Suffering unto God," trans. J. Matthew Ashley, *Critical Inquiry* 20, no. 4 (Summer 1994): 615.

13. In my approach to contemplative photography, I follow Andy Karr and Michael Wood. See their main work, *The Practice of Contemplative Photography: Seeing the World with Fresh Eyes* (Boulder, CO: Shambhala Publications, 2011); see also their website, accessed December 30, 2016, http://seeingfresh.com/galleries/andy-karr-and-michael-wood.

14. Sebastiao Salgado, *From My Land to the Planet* (Milan, Italy: Contrasto, 2014), 4.

15. Beth Moon, *Ancient Trees: Portraits of Time* (New York: Abbeville Press, 2014).

16. Gretchen Gardner, *Gerry Sharpe, Sun and Shade: A Photographer's Story* (Columbus, OH: Ohio State University Press, 2012), 63.

17. Paul Caponigro, *Dark into Light*, Gallery catalogue (Boston: Pucker Gallery, 2015), 16.

18. See Ansel Adams, "Frozen Lake and Cliffs," in *Examples, the Making of 40 photographs*, 11–13.

19. As an example of the fruit of the experience of missing mercy, consider the experience of Friedrich von Spee, who from the depths of despair wrote one of the most popular German Advent songs at the time of the inquisition and the burning of witches. Identifying with Isaiah's prophetic, quasi-apocalyptic call: "O Heiland reiss die Himmel auf…." ("O Savior, Rend the Heavens"), von Spee cried to heaven in the situation of the burning of the innocent in the name of the church.

20. I am using here Matt Ashley's translation of Metz's phrase, *Leiden an Gott*, as "Suffering *unto* God; see "In Place of a Foreword / Introduction: Reading Metz," n19, in A *Passion for God: The Mystical-Political Dimension of Christianity*, trans. J. Matthew Ashley (Mahwah, NJ: Paulist Press, 1998), 177–78.

21. William Herzog, *Parables as Subversive Speech: Jesus as Pedagogue of the Oppressed* (Louisville, KY: Westminster/John Knox Press, 1994); Luise Schottroff, *The Parables of Jesus*, trans. L. Maloney (Minneapolis: Fortress Press, 2006).

22. See Schottroff, *The Parables of Jesus*, 210–16; Herzog, *Parables as Subversive Speech*, 79, 95.

23. The use of the term *apocalyptic* springs from the central question raised by the lament tradition of the Old Testament: "How long?" How long will the oppression last? How long must we endure killing and violence? How long the suffering? Metz summarizes these questions under the category of "Asking God back" (*Rückfragen an Gott*) that can be translated as "turning one's questioning back to God," or "insistent questioning of God;" see note 19 to J. Matthew Ashley's "Introduction" to Metz, A *Passion for God*, 177–78. This "asking God back" is profoundly connected to the Biblical lament tradition; see Julia D. E. Prinz, *Endangering Hunger for God* (Münster: Lit-Verlag, 2006), 159. This central apocalyptic question becomes an eschatological dimension of the New Testament. See the use of "eschatological interpretation" by Luise Schottroff for each parable in her work, *Parables of Jesus*. On the central importance of the apocalyptic framework for Christology, see Metz's "Untimely Theses on Apocalyptic" in chap. 10 of Metz, *Faith in History and Society*, especially theses XXII–XXIX, 162–63.

24. Metz, "Caro cardo salutis," 174.

25. Ibid., 169.

26. See Metz, "The Future Seen from the Memory of Suffering," *Faith in History and Society*, 97–113.

27. Metz, "In Place of a Foreword: On the Biographical Itinerary of My Theology," *A Passion for God*, 2.

28. Metz, "Theology as Theodicy?" *A Passion for God*, 68. It is in the context of his treatment of mourning, lamentation, and the absence of God that Metz asks, "Is such a sense of absence at all consoling?" See "A Passion for God: Religious Orders Today," *A Passion for God*, 160.

29. Metz, "Caro cardo salutis," 178. "In this body our final image has been unfolded" is my translation of "der Leib selbst ist der Schicksalsraum, in dem und aus dem unsere Ewigkeit sich aufbaut."

2

What Do I Stand For?

Francis of Assisi and the Anthropological Revolution

John K. Downey

My colleague returned home from the university one afternoon to find her husband tending their large garden. "So," she remarked to him, "you've put in a statue of St. Francis." "Oh," replied her husband, "is that what it is? I thought it was a scarecrow." It is not always clear what we are talking about when we talk about Francis.[1]

Francesco di Bernadone was born around 1181 in Italy.[2] He was a "rich kid" whose father had made good money selling expensive imported cloth. Francis was an ordinary young man in his late teens and early twenties. He shared his wealth with his young friends, dressed well, and was a good dancer and singer. In fact, he became president of the local *Tripudianti*—what we might call the "Assisi Club for Drinking, Dancing, and Pranks." He fought in a war against the nearby city of Perugia and spent a terrible year as a prisoner of war. When he returned home, he was restless and unhappy. As with many of us, facing death and suffering had brought him face-to-face with the question of what it means to have a worthwhile life, how to make it worth living rather than just living. He did eventually find his direction and discover what he stood for.

Francis became poor to call us to a richer humanity, one centered on our connection to God and to others. He comes to us in the stories and memories that testify to the core of his vision. In these we find him reminding us that we are connected sons and daughters of the creator—and we should act like it. Simple, yet these stories can also be misunderstood and limited to superficial points. This misunderstanding is one reason we need theological reflection as well as spiritual record: to sharpen the borders and the message of our religious experiences and grounding narratives. The new political theology of Johann Baptist Metz proves an excellent companion to the spiritual experience of Francesco. Metz's theological narrative springs from a similar grounding in suffering and solidarity; it also demands acting, not just believing, and flows from the human being and God in relationship. The call to penance or conversion in Francis is described by Metz as an anthropological revolution, a change of heart, in which a new vision of what it means to be human takes hold:

> It is not a liberation from our powerlessness, but from our own form of predominance. It frees us, not from the state of being dominated but from that of dominating; not from our sufferings but from our apathy; not from guilt but from our innocence.[3]

This revolution damages our self-interest and reorganizes our habitual way of life. It is what we talk about when we talk about mercy.

Two stories about the young twentysomething Francis may indicate the shape of his thinking.[4] One day, as he roamed about, he wandered into an old, dilapidated church, San Damiano, and prayed before the crucifix there. We are told that this cross seemed to speak to him, "Francis, repair my church. Can't you see it is falling into ruin?" He immediately began to scrub the bricks and repair the walls. But then he had what we might call his "Homer Simpson" moment: "D'oh!" He realized that the voice was not telling him to repair the physical bricks of a church but the spiritual mission of the church itself.[5]

Later, he saw that for him this mission of repair meant living a dedicated religious life. To do this he needed to renounce his right to the family fortune. His father had Francis called up on charges before the bishop for selling off expensive cloth and a horse and giving away the proceeds. The court was held in the piazza in front of the bishop's residence, in the presence of the entire town. The bishop told Francis to give back his father's money. Francis agreed, but he also took off each layer of his fine clothing—including his underwear. "From now on I will say freely: 'Our Father who art in heaven,' and not 'My father, Pietro di Bernadone.'"[6] The naked Francis was covered by the cape of the bishop and left in a worker's tunic. Now he would start a new life of giving thanks to and trusting in God.

Francis decided he must live a life of radical trust in God and others. But Francis never scolded; he simply said this is how he must live. Formerly wealthy, now a beggar, Francis had found what he stood for. Oddly, his way hit a chord: many young men gave their money away and joined him. By the time of his death, he had thousands of followers. He spoke to the needs of his times. In his time, money was returning to use and causing confusion about how to relate to wealth in the new shape of movable money rather than immovable land. His were times of great violence, wars among citizens over power and freedom. The social structures were shifting with the rise of a mercantile class challenging the propertied aristocrats. The shifting social hierarchy replaced the earlier stability that had provided security. Are we so different? No, we are not medieval, but we do hope for a life with meaning and value. We too live in times of conflict and violence; we too are unsure how to relate to money, and we too are unsure of what counts as a meaningful place in society.

Johann Baptist Metz is no medieval spiritual master, yet he too sees we must drill down and repair our basic orientation. He too wants to ask who we are in this cosmos. For both Metz and Francis, we have a responsibility before God to recognize our brothers and sisters—however different they may be. Both men do this by becoming sensitive to the suffering of others. To use the jargon of Metz, both men want to construct a horizon for living that is mystical, because it includes religious experience, and political, because it looks to the concrete social setting of our lived humanity in culture, economics, and the vectors of power.

Metz himself tells two stories about the biographical grounding of his development of a political theology. He was drafted into the German army near the end of World War II when he was just sixteen years old. After he returned from the war, he asked his mother and the other members of his family what they thought about the horrible camps for Jews that Hitler had operated. They said they knew nothing about these. What did they mean? He had no reason to doubt their sincerity, but how could this much suffering go on and people not know? Even more troubling was his experience at the front. His company commander sent him back to headquarters with a message. When he returned to his company the next morning, he found them all dead. A bombing raid and tanks had left only the lifeless bodies of his comrades. He wandered around for days "with a soundless cry": Why?

For Metz, even today the main question of theology and religion is the question of God and human suffering (theodicy): Why do others suffer? How are they saved? There is also the question of how we can speak of humanity in the face of human suffering inflicted and endured in places such as Auschwitz. For him, the touchstone for theological analysis today is *memoria passionis*, a memory of suffering, which comes to expression in an engaged compassion. It is not enough for reason to focus on data and technical skills; reason must be directed to the human good, to the value of others. Francis too wants us to reorient our lives and challenges us to open our eyes to the suffering of others.

The poverty of Francis—precisely because he had been a wealthy man—brings the suffering of the truly poor into view and sparks compassion among his peers. Francis offers a God-consciousness that calls people to act because they are valued and connected to the rest of the universe. In this way, the story of Francis can be what Metz calls a dangerous memory. It also offers us an anthropology of solidarity that impels us to resist indifference. Metz puts it this way: "There are dangerous memories, memories that make demands on us. There are memories in which earlier experiences break through to the center point of our lives and reveal new and dangerous insights for the present. They are memories we have to consider; memories, as it were, with future content."[7] Both Francis of Assisi and Johann Baptist Metz want human beings to remember who they are in the cosmos and to act accordingly. To bring home the danger of Francis, I want to take up the two foci used by his early biographer, Thomas of Celano: incarnation and compassion.[8]

INCARNATION

Nothing is more striking to Francis than the Christian doctrine of the incarnation. He could not get over the image of God becoming a human being. God loved him, loved us, so much that he came to be with us in a form that is weak and poor. For Francis, this act of humility and graciousness became the model and inspiration for a Christian universe and for discipleship: to be like Jesus is to empty ourselves of a focus on ourselves and embrace those who are "other." This is how the Word is made flesh. This is the poverty of the incarnation.

In 1223, in the tiny village of Greccio at Christmas, Francis brought in a manger and real animals. "For I wish to enact the memory of that babe who was born in Bethlehem: to see as much as possible with my own bodily eyes the discomfort of his infant needs, how he lay in a manger, and how with an ox and an ass standing by, he rested on hay." Book 1 of Celano's *Life of Francis* ends with and is summed up by this Christmas scene, the incarnation of God in the birth of Jesus Christ as a naked baby. "There simplicity is given a place of honor, poverty is exalted, humility is commended, and out of Greccio is made a new Bethlehem."[9] If little Greccio can be a place of the incarnation, then certainly your hometown can be.

Nakedness surrounded the life of Francis. At the beginning of his new life, Francis stripped off his clothes and declared loyalty only to his father in heaven. His life ended with his request to be placed naked on the ground when he died. His model was the Christ who lowered himself to be swaddled in an animal feeding trough. The incarnation is a move of vulnerability and generosity. To be vulnerable is to have no defense or control and to trust others; it is to be naked. This poverty of the incarnation is not a denial of our good world—which is a wonderful gift. Rather, the poverty of Jesus's incarnation is a poverty of acting to enrich others. For Francis, poverty was not about what you do not have, but about using what you have been given for others. Defining the self through control and possession moves one into a logic of domination.[10] Turning away from this anthropology is the point of the various ascetical tactics of humility that Francis practiced. Fasting, begging, living poorly, attending first to others' needs, disciplining the ego and the body—all these encourage right relations with the self, God, and others. Francis and the brothers are unique in their call to extreme social and physical measures of the practice of poverty, but all Christians are called to live the God-centered life of dependence and relationship. This is the poverty of Francis: being there for others.

Finding human dignity through the incarnation amounts to an anthropological revolution for Metz. This revolution is "our attempt to achieve a new relationship to ourselves, to our natural and social environment, which is not one of domination and exploitation."[11] It is in living a life of genuine vulnerability, nakedness, and dependence—in the decentering of our ego, in accepting a certain lack of control—that Christians discover the God of Jesus. Metz argues that this sort of humility, this poverty of spirit, brings human limits into view and affirms human transcendence in the relationship to God and humankind. Political theology is thereby rooted in faithfulness to being human. "To become human means to become 'poor,' to have nothing that one might brag about before God."[12] The transcendent captivates and interrupts, but it also shows us our dignity and duty. Nothing belongs to us—not extra money beyond what we truly need, not titles, not our talents. What comes from God must not be possessed by us but used for others.

Control and subjugation are not what make one human. Metz cautions against living off a "bread of domination" that disconnects people: subjugation does not give lives their value. "An identity thus formed through the principles of domination and subjugation makes the individual profoundly disconnected and, in the strict sense of the term, egoistic."[13] To be human is to realize connectedness, responsibility, and vulnerability. Moreover, this false anthropology of domination leads to the attempt to dominate even death. But the real threat to humanity is not death but the denial of death. As Metz observes,

> It is, in fact, not death itself which alienates us from ourselves and snatches life from us: it is, instead, the suppression of death, the flight from death. This suppression of death has made us into those dominating beings bent on subjugation who today are everywhere encountering the limits of their survival.[14]

Francis of Assisi reflects a similar anthropology. Francis was not alienated from death. In his *Canticle of the Creatures*, he gives praise and thanks for all of nature—including "Sister Death."

Francis was disturbing: he challenged the way things were and lived his life differently. He did not accept the status society gave him as a rich man, but begged and wore rags. He did not participate in the culture of money and forbade the brothers from even touching it. He did not want a house, but would rather be a pilgrim. He was not satisfied with what was

What Do I Stand For?

normal. In the first line of his *Testament,* he says, "The Lord gave me, Brother Francis, thus to begin doing penance in this way." But penance means conversion, "a wholly new way of seeing reality—a new way of seeing himself, others, the world, and God himself" that entails new values and behaviors.[15]

Metz puts it this way: the shortest definition of religion is interruption.[16] Christian discipleship calls for disruption of the futures we have made for ourselves by what may come. It is about moving beyond apathy, egoism, and control. This *metanoia,* this conversion, this change of heart calls humankind to a new future that will repair the crumbling church, the church that is not meeting the needs of its people. When we cease moving within a culture of domination and move to a culture of recognition and solidarity, we set a new framework for what it means to be human. This new anthropology is not about having more or controlling more, but about compassion. This conversion, as Metz says, goes through people like a shock, reaching deep down into the direction of their lives, into established systems of needs and desires. "It damages and disrupts our immediate self-interest and aims at a fundamental reorganization of our habitual way of life."[17] In the end, it is how we live that reveals our grounding and recommends that relationship to others. Similarly, Celano sums up Francis: "He filled the whole world with the gospel of Christ...proclaiming to everyone the good news of the kingdom of God, edifying his listeners by his example as much as by his words, as he made of his whole body a tongue."[18]

In his *Admonitions,* Francis talks about St. Paul's dictum that "the letter kills but the spirit gives life." In one sense, Francis read the gospel rather literally, but finally he read it for the spirit, not the letter. And to him, finding the spirit meant doing, making the incarnation a way of living.[19] As Francis says in his letter to the Third Order (lay associates of the Friars),

> We are spouses when the faithful soul is united by the Holy Spirit to our Lord Jesus Christ. We are brothers, moreover, when we do the will of His Father Who is in heaven; mothers when we carry Him in our heart and body through love and a pure and sincere conscience; and give Him birth through a holy activity, which must shine before others by example.[20]

45

For Metz, too, human connectedness makes ethical claims and Christians are called to show their connection in their actions. "Ultimately, it is of the very essence of the Christian faith to be believed in such a way that it is never just believed, but rather—in the messianic praxis of discipleship—enacted."[21] Celano's *Lives of Saint Francis* declares that, for Francis, "words do not do what is good, they only point to it."[22]

The surprising window to God's future and covenant opens when we see the suffering of others. Jesus followed his Jewish tradition by joining the love of God to the love of neighbor. And this means that human beings are not the autonomous controlling center of their lives; rather they are in relation. Remembering who we are brings us to a sense of connectedness in our vulnerability. Responding to the love of God turns the human heart outward. The memory of Christ does not lead to ecstatic removal from a tainted world, but to kissing lepers.

COMPASSION

This incarnation that attacks egocentrism demands that human beings turn outward: incarnation entails solidarity. For Francis, God's creatures were literally brothers and sisters, and this fact compelled a response of gratitude and brotherhood. And the imitation of Christ calls Christians to solidarity. Francis hated and feared lepers. Yet one day he was moved to embrace one of them. Francis's hugging the leper triggered a conversion, a turning point: he realized the leper he had hugged was a fellow creature of God, a brother. "For when I was in sin, it seemed too bitter for me to see lepers....And when I left them, what had seemed bitter to me was turned to sweetness of soul and body."[23]

Doing penance has a practical intent; conversion means doing something, changing the way one lives one's life because that life is reordered.[24] As he says, "I showed mercy to them."[25] Mercy is not a subtle mode of domination or self-importance; it is not a one-way street trodden by the giver. The Latin in the original is *"faci misericordiam cum illis,"* which is literally rendered as "I made mercy with them." Mercy names the acting out of our kinship. Francis, in his *Testament*, highlights this moment as the conversion point in his life.[26] The recognition of lepers as human beings changed his life. And his doing mercy reintegrated lepers into human society.[27]

To find God, Francis had to move beyond himself. Those who constituted the least in Assisi, the invisible ones, are the litmus test of human dignity and worth. This realization changed everything: it demanded a distance from the exploitation of others inherent in the emerging monetary system, from warfare that kills, and from the private property that tells them they are not as worthy. What needs to be fixed is the person's relationship to fellow creatures; what needs to stop is the fracturing of the human community. Perhaps this is why Francis was "in sin" before that transformative encounter with a leper: "The Lord gave me, Brother Francis, thus to begin doing penance in this way: for when I was in sin, it seemed too bitter for me to see lepers."[28] Our lives are out of joint—bitter and misdirected—when we do not recognize the other as our brother or sister.

Consider the harmony called for in what is, after all, called the *Canticle of the Creatures* and that also includes praise for pardoning others. One theme of Francis is certainly reconciliation and ending conflict. He cast out demons in Arezzo; he made peace between the hungry wolf and people of Gubbio; he traveled to visit the Sultan al-Malik al-Kamil, who was leading the Muslim forces against the Crusaders. In the *Canticle*, the entire world—sun, moon, fire, water, weather—is at one in praising God. But humankind may resist. In the second to last stanza, we hear, "Praised be You, my Lord, through those who give pardon for Your love."[29] We are exhorted to embrace harmony with others. Making mercy is the key to the incarnation that brings solidarity and completes the cosmic hymn.

In hearing the voices of the marginal, of those who have disappeared in our social calculus, we find ourselves. We come to "sweetness" in being liberated from a drive to deny our human community under God. Metz observes similarly, "To speak of this God means to speak of the suffering of the stranger and to lament responsibility neglected and solidarity denied."[30] As Augustine puts it, sin is turning the heart inward. As we have seen, in political theology Christianity becomes a challenge to live a new anthropology: to recognize our responsibility and to act in solidarity. It is founded on a hope that the human heart will turn outward. As Metz puts it, Christianity is a "community of memory and narrative in imitation of Jesus, a community of those who looked first to the suffering of others."[31] He opposes any privatized or individualized notion of Christian life. Conversion and mysticism are public and community affairs. For him, the Christian life is a life together, not a personal salvation. "Only when our hope is inseparable from hope for others, in other words, only when it automatically assumes the form and motion of love and communion, does it cease to be petty and fearful, a hopeless reflection of our egotism."[32] He focuses this concern by pointing to the parable of the Good Samaritan.

The biblical story of the Good Samaritan turns on the least likely person helping his least favorite person. A Jew is robbed, beaten, and thrown in a ditch. His Jewish brothers and leaders pass him by, but a Samaritan does not. For us today, a Samaritan is a good person who helps you change your flat tire on the freeway. But in the time of Jesus, the Samaritan group was a hated religious and political enemy. For Jesus, there is a surprise, a reorienting experience, in mercy. Christians don't get to decide who is the neighbor—the person about whom they should care or from whom they might receive care; our neighbor is whoever is there. The biblical tradition preaches a type of universal responsibility. For Metz, as for Francis, Christianity is a community that sees and embraces others—even aliens and enemies. "People who use 'God' the way Jesus does accept the violation of their own personal preconceived certainties by the misfortune of others."[33] This authority of the others' suffering cannot so easily be deflated by defining others as "them" or glossed over in the oblivion of a theory. The incarnation draws one into the dynamic of compassion. Francis had already learned from the lepers that members of the human community "were sacred creatures of God and that every attitude and action that does violence to this sacred community must be repented of."[34]

Jesus's suffering compels people to engage the suffering of others in the world. The story of Francesco emerges as mystical and political, that is, a story of the incarnation and compassion of Christ and his followers lived in historical, social, and cultural relations. The cry of the victims, the voice of the other, must be heard. Francis of Assisi preached a God-consciousness that disrupts alienation, conflict, and domination with social responsibility and communion. This consciousness amounts to an anthropological revolution, a new way of being human, given to us in our experience of incarnation and compassion. We come to be grounded in mercy.

TWICE BLESSED: STANDING FOR MERCY

Words conjure a world. Words help us to remember where we stand. Francis of Assisi offered us a new world framed by a call for incarnation and compassion. Johann Baptist Metz uses the language of the anthropological revolution and the injection of the dangerous memory of suffering into human living. Who is our neighbor? Who is our brother and sister? Who are the lepers? Mercy brings these questions to the fore. There is something surprising about mercy. When we use that word, we expect that things will be askew, different from business as usual. Sometimes one talks about mercy when legal justice becomes more generous or when magnanimity overcomes the right to kill or damage someone, when a gracious consideration is given to others, or when the usual rules do not apply. But mercy is more than a single act: it describes the grounding vision from which we act; it is what we stand for.[35]

There is, then, for us both as human beings and as Christians a duty to live in a culture of mercy. The word can have many uses, but here I want only to claim that *mercy* can be shorthand for the dangerous memory, the anthropological revolution, of Francis. It is about overcoming whatever makes the different one invisible. It is about compassion. It is about making mercy with lepers and pardoning those with whom we are fighting. It is about seeing with the eyes of mercy. This mercy would not be a covert form of control that makes others less and puts them in my debt. It would not be a cynical way to project personal power. But we are twice blessed in the divine and human act of solidarity with the daughters and sons of our Father. And this is a duty that precedes any laws of economics or group loyalty. It is a personal connection and response to the authority of the suffering of others in which we act with different goals in mind. We've had a change of heart. We need to be scared away from the risky individualism pervading our politics, economics, and technology.

This spirituality is a responsibility to live in the world. Francis offered a way of thinking about money, status, and power that was a sort of economic and social foolishness. We have a thread in our society today, as he did then, that wishes to say the poor really are not as human as the rest of us—they are lazy and unworthy. We don't see them as like us—just as Francis saw the lepers before his conversion. There is leadership that reduces others to dehumanized submission. There are those whose trading and dealing in business only subtract from the wealth of the common good and only benefit them and theirs.[36] But for Francis, all good things are from God and are not ours; they are given to us so that we enrich others in imitation of the incarnation. As Metz would remind us, we need to see the suffering of others, to have the Samaritan response. Xenophobia, racism, misogyny, and religiously tinged nationalism are traps that shrivel our religious and human selves.[37] What do our actions and beliefs say that we stand for?

Francis's actions remind believers who they are—and are not. They are heralds of a great king, but they are not the King. They are creatures who, like all creatures, praise God by being what they are. They are kin.[38] To Francis, relationships matter. The human person emerges in vulnerability and humility that call for dependence on God and others. This incarnational duty and our call to compassion are intertwined with a sensitivity to suffering. This is the new revolutionary ground as human beings and creatures. It provides the horizon within which we act and hope.

In his *Canticle*, Francis poses the question of whether we today can accept the familial world that God has given to us.[39] Compassion and incarnation require a deep down revolution. "Is there any suffering at all in the world of which we might say that it does not concern us at all? Is there a single cry of suffering that is not meant for every ear?"[40] This is the question only mercy can answer.

NOTES

1. Our words do not have their meanings built into them. Looking at actual texts of Francis with a critical theological eye provides some control for interpretation. For an example of the dangers, see the use of Francis to champion Fascism as documented by Amanda Minervini in "Face to Face: Iconic Representations and Juxtapositions of St. Francis of Assisi and Mussolini during Italian Fascism," in M. Epstein, F. Orsitto, A. Righi, eds., *Tot Art: The Visual Arts, Fascism(s), and Mass-Society* (Cambridge: Cambridge Scholars Publishing, 2017).

2. The best new biography is André Vauchez, *Francis of Assisi: The Life and Afterlife of a Medieval Saint* (New Haven, CT: Yale University Press, 2012). For a brief introduction to Francis, see the review of two recent Francis biographies by Joan Acocella, "Rich Man, Poor Man: The Radical Vision of St. Francis," *The New Yorker*, January 14, 2013, 72–77.

3. Johann Baptist Metz, "Bread of Survival: The Lord's Supper of Christians as Anticipatory Sign of an Anthropological Revolution," in *Love's Strategy: The Political Theology of Johann Baptist Metz*, ed. John K. Downey (Harrisburg, PA: Trinity Press International, 1999), 60.

4. With Francis we have memory and story recorded in a few works by him and then early biographical—hagiographical—sources. References to the historical texts, including Thomas of Celano's *Lives of Saint Francis* (*The Life of Saint Francis*, *The Remembrance of the Desire of a Soul*, and *The Treatise on the Miracles of Saint Francis*) as well as the *Testament*, the *Canticle of the Creatures*, and other writings of Francis himself are to the critical edition of Franciscan texts in the three volumes of *Francis of Assisi: Early Documents*, ed. Regis J. Armstrong, J. A. Wayne Hellmann, and William J. Short, vol. 1, *The Saint*; vol. 2, *The Founder*; vol. 3, *The Prophet* (New York: New City Press, 1999–2001). Citations to these translations are to verse numbers unless otherwise stated.

5. Thomas of Celano, *Remembrance of the Desire of a Soul*, 10. Hereafter, *Remembrance*. For another story of how Francis, like us, can misunderstand his experience of God, see his dream about a house full of armor in Celano, *Remembrance*, 6.

6. Celano, *Remembrance*, 12.

7. Johann Baptist Metz, "The Future in the Memory of Suffering," in Johann Baptist Metz and Jürgen Moltmann, *Faith and the Future: Essays on Theology, Solidarity, and Modernity* (Maryknoll, NY: Orbis Books, 1995), 8.

8. Brother Thomas of Celano collected stories about Francis and presented his biography, *The Life of Saint Francis*, in 1229. Hereafter, *Life*. He wrote another life of Francis, *The Remembrance of the Desire of a Soul*, in 1247.

9. Celano, *Life*, 84–85.

10. Metz, "1492," 13: "His logic became a logic of domination, not of recognition: a logic of assimilation and not of otherness."

11. Metz, "Bread of Survival," 60.

12. Johann Baptist Metz, *Poverty of Spirit*, trans. John Drury (Mahwah, NJ: Paulist Press, 1998), 10.

13. Metz, "Bread of Survival," 54.

14. Ibid., 56.

15. Michael F. Cusato, "To Do Penance/*Facere poenitentiam*," *The Cord* 57 (February/March 2007): 3–24, at 9.

16. Johann Baptist Metz, *Faith in History and Society: Toward a Practical Fundamental Theology*, trans. J. Matthew Ashley (New York: Crossroad Publishing Co., 2007), 158.

17. Metz, "Bread of Survival," 60.

18. Celano, *Life*, 97.

19. Francis of Assisi, *Admonitions*, 132.

20. Francis of Assisi, *Later Admonitions and Exhortations*, 51–53.

21. Metz, "Christians and Jews after Auschwitz," *Love's Strategy*, 47.

22. Celano, *Life*, 93.

23. Francis of Assisi, *Testament*, par. 1.

24. See Raffaele Pazzelli, *St. Francis and the Third Order: The Franciscan and pre-Franciscan Penitential Movement* (Chicago, IL: Franciscan Herald Press, 1989), 120–37.

25. *Testament*, par. 1.

26. For more background on this conversion, see Michael Higgins, TOR, "*Dominus conduxit me inter illos, et feci misericordiam cum illis* (Test 2): Francis of Assisi and Mercy." *Franciscan Studies* 64 (2006): 17–32.

27. Vauchez, *Francis of Assisi*, 24–25.

28. *Testament*, par. 1. Remember that "the sight of lepers was so bitter to him that…even two miles away he would cover his nose with his hands" (Celano, *Life*, 17). Celano continues, "When he started thinking of holy and useful matters with the grace and strength of the Most High, while in the clothes of the world, he met a leper one day. Made stronger than himself, he came up and kissed him. He then began to consider himself less and less."

29. Francis of Assisi, *Canticle of the Creatures*, 12–13. We are told that the mayor and the bishop were in angry contention. When Francis had some brothers sing his *Canticle*, and this verse especially, for them, they forgave each other.

30. Johann Baptist Metz, "In the Pluralism of Religious and Cultural Worlds: Notes Toward a Theological and Political Program," trans. John K. Downey and Heiko Wiggers, *Love's Strategy*, 170. "Every

authentic religious act is directed toward the concreteness of God in our human neighbors and their world. There it finds its living fulfillment and its transcendent point of contact. Could humanity be taken any more seriously than that? Is anything more radically anthropocentric than God's creative love?" (Metz, *Poverty of Spirit*, 32–33).

31. Metz, "Pluralism," 169.

32. Metz, "Communicating a Dangerous Memory," *Love's Strategy*, 138.

33. Metz, "Pluralism," 170.

34. Michael F. Cusato, "The Mystical Experience behind the Stigmatization Narrative," *The Stigmata of Francis of Assisi: New Studies, New Perspectives* (St. Bonaventure, NY: Franciscan Institute, 2006), 29–74, at 73. The suffering of Jesus, as with the suffering of Francis, points us to compassion for others.

35. Such a foundation would radically alter our actions and perceptions. See, e.g., the church as Jon Sobrino imagines if its marks were to be one, holy, catholic, apostolic—and now merciful: "The Samaritan Church and the Principle of Mercy," in Jon Sobrino, *The Principle of Mercy: Taking the Crucified People from the Cross* (Maryknoll, NY: Orbis Books, 1994), 15–26.

36. Francis was no economist, but there are implications for economic theory. See Giacomo Todeschini, *Franciscan Wealth: From Voluntary Poverty to Market Society* (St. Bonaventure, NY: The Franciscan Institute, 2009).

37. Metz, "Pluralism," 174–75.

38. See, Celano, *Life*, 16, and the *Canticle of the Creatures*. People as different from Francis as a leper or a Sultan remain sisters and brothers. For a well-drawn discussion of this connectedness that also looks at the role of conversion, see Cusato, "To Do Penance," esp. 11–24.

39. Jacques Dalarum, *The Canticle of Brother Sun: Francis of Assisi Reconciled*, trans. Philippe Yates (St. Bonaventure, NY: Franciscan Institute, 2016), 100.

40. Johann Baptist Metz, "The Last Universalists," in *The Future of Theology: Essays in Honor of Jürgen Moltmann*, ed. Miroslav Volf, Carmen Krieg, and Thomas Kucharz,, trans. Douglas Scott (Grand Rapids, MI: William B. Eerdmans, 1996), 51.

II

INTERRUPTION

3

"Time, the Mercy of the Messiah"

Pope Francis and Johann Baptist Metz

Michael Kirwan, SJ

INTRODUCTION: "TIME IS THE MERCY OF ETERNITY"

In his writings, and in many addresses and homilies, Pope Francis has followed the distinctive theological style, the *teología del pueblo* ("theology of the people") of his native Argentina—best understood as a local variant on Latin American liberation theology. This chapter will attempt to compare this style with key themes from the postwar political theology of Johann Baptist Metz, whom we can think of as liberation theology's "European cousin." A full-length study of the resemblances between Metz and Francis would be fascinating, but I will limit myself to one theme: a comparison of their perspectives on *time*. Metz stresses the importance of "Messianic time," while Francis urges a pastoral theological imperative: "Time is greater than space."

What Pope Francis understands by time's priority over space is not always crystal clear. The aphorism is one of four pastoral theological priorities adopted by Jorge Bergoglio as provincial of the Jesuits, and then as archbishop of Buenos Aires, by way of guidelines toward the common good. He stresses, first, the priority of *time* over space;

57

second, the priority of *unity* over conflict; third, the priority of *reality* over the idea; and fourth, the superiority of the *whole* over the parts (that is, the whole is more than the mere sum of the parts).[1] But it does appear that the first of these principles has an especially strong significance for him.

I would suggest that its significance is beautifully conveyed if we consider another aphorism, from the English poet and mystic William Blake (1757–1827). A key struggle for Blake—or, we might say, the knot he was trying to untie—was how to reconcile his fierce libertarian antinomianism (which he shared with other poets of the Romantic age) and his intense fascination with the person of the forgiving Christ. Blake set these two qualities—Romantic revolutionary energy and Christian orthodoxy—in fierce tension with one another, in a satirical work titled *The Marriage of Heaven and Hell* (1793). The poem includes a chapter containing the "Proverbs of Hell," one of which runs "Time is the Mercy of Eternity."

The proverb expresses superbly the tenor of Francis's pastorally oriented theological wisdom, not least in the Jubilee Year of Mercy in 2015–16. A link between "time" and "mercy" is implicit in Pope Francis's motto, *Miserando atque Eligendo* ("By having mercy and by choosing him"), which he comments on in an interview with Antonio Spadaro.[2] The phrase is taken from St. Bede's commentary on the call of Matthew in Matthew 9 and points out the conflation of two events that we normally think of as consecutive. First, the experience of forgiveness makes possible the vocation to follow Christ in living mercifully. In the example of the summons of Matthew, however, the declaration of forgiveness and the call to discipleship are, so to speak, one and the same "speech-act."

We need to realize, as did Blake, that "mercy" is a much wider category than "forgiveness of sins." If we simply equate *mercy* with absolution or the remission of wrongdoing, we impoverish the term and we are in danger of missing the rich significance of what Pope Francis is trying to say.

In *Evangelii Gaudium*, Pope Francis asserts that to begin "processes that build up a people in history" is a more important task than to occupy positions (*espacios*) of power, or possession of land or wealth (nos. 223, 224).[3] He remarks that "time governs spaces, illumines them, and makes them links in a constantly expanding chain, with no possibility of return." Likewise, in his World Youth Day homily in Rio de Janeiro in 2013, Pope Francis declares, "God is real. He manifests himself today. God is everywhere."[4] He reiterates the historical nature of this revelation:

> Time initiates processes, and space crystallizes them. God is in history, in the processes. We must not focus on occupying the spaces where power is exercised, but rather on starting long-run historical processes. We must initiate processes rather than occupy spaces. God manifests himself in time and is present in the processes of history. This gives priority to actions that give birth to new historical dynamics. And it requires patience, waiting.[5]

It would be interesting to know what the jubilant young people on Copacabana Beach made of Francis's cryptic declaration that "time initiates processes, and space crystallizes them!" Philosophically at least, the notion is richly suggestive. His insistence on locating God's revelation in the "processes of history" is consonant with the "classic" liberationist view, such as we find in Gustavo Gutiérrez's A *Theology of Liberation*.[6] Francis distances his approach from determinist Marxism, but he never in any sense downplays the appeal to "history" as the arena of transformation.

The claim that "time is greater than space" recurs in the 2016 postsynodal exhortation *Amoris Laetitia* (The Joy of Loving). The Synod on the Family was seeking to respond to the challenge to the Christian ideal of marriage posed by relationships that do not correspond to it: the divorced and remarried, couples married civilly or cohabiting, and those in same-sex unions. Francis warns of two dangers: first, an "immoderate desire for total change" that is not grounded on in-depth reflection, and second, a rigorist attitude that looks to resolve pastoral problems by a simple mechanical application of general rules. Neither of these is adequate: the antidote to both is stated in what follows: "Since 'time is greater than space,' I would make it clear that not all discussions of doctrinal, moral or pastoral issues need to be settled by interventions of the magisterium" (no. 3).[7]

The maxim is presented, therefore, as a pastoral principle that justifies the restraint of the teaching authority from making interventions, to nurture a discussion that will avoid excessive laxity on the one hand, and excessive rigor on the other. Francis elaborates in several ways, even when the principle is only implicit. For example, he has described the church as having sometimes to act as a "field hospital." The image first appears in the Spadaro interview, where the most urgent task of the church is "the ability to heal wounds and to warm the hearts of the faithful; it needs nearness, proximity":

> I see the church as a field hospital after battle. It is useless to ask a seriously injured person if he has high cholesterol and about the level of his blood sugars! You have to heal his wounds. Then we can talk about everything else. Heal the wounds, heal the wounds....The Good Samaritan washes, cleans and raises up his neighbor. This is pure Gospel.[8]

There is a crucial difference between a critically wounded patient in need of emergency aid and the same patient convalescing from those injuries. Time makes a difference.

The image recurs in *Amoris Laetitia* (see no. 291). Two further themes from this document will be considered below: *seeds of the Word* and *gradualness* in pastoral care—each requiring an attitude of spiritual discernment. These emphasize the temporal dimension of pastoral accompaniment, reinforcing, once again, the priority of time as "the mercy of Eternity."

FRANCIS AND THE *TEOLOGÍA DEL PUEBLO*

A few words of introduction to the distinctively Argentinian *teología del pueblo*, so influential on Pope Francis, may be in order. It is identified by the theologian Juan Carlos Scannone as one of a number of streams of Latin American liberation theology, distinguished from the others by its emphasis on the use of cultural analysis rather than the social sciences. Alternatively referred to as "populist theology" and "popular pastoral theology," it would not be unjust to describe it as a predominantly (but not exclusively) Argentinian variant of liberation theology.[9]

El pueblo (the people) is defined not in terms of their oppressed status within an unjust social economic structure, but as a group with its own wisdom accumulated in popular culture. *El pueblo* is different from "the masses" because it has acquired a social consciousness. "It is the subject of a history (memory, consciousness and historical project) and a common culture,"[10] therefore, it has common goals and an ability to work toward the common good.

Scannone gives a historical example, the Tinkunaco fiesta of La Rioja in Argentina, to show how popular religion can be a vehicle of transformative religious meaning. This New Year festival consists in a ritualized encounter between St. Nicholas (representing the indigenous people) and the child mayor, *el niño alcade* (who stands for the Spanish colonial authorities). It joyfully commemorates an altercation in the late fifteenth century between the two groups—two cultures— that was resolved peacefully. Scannone notes the significance of this story and its commemoration:

> Both the rite and the legend tacitly demand, through their symbols, a just social peace in which preference is given to the poorest and most oppressed, those who gather beside the Mayor Niño. In addition, the Tinkunaco symbolically confesses that all political authority comes from God and must be exercised for the common good, with special care for those who are victims of injustice.[11]

This is a popular expression, as it were, of the "eschatological proviso" described by Metz. In the words of Agnes Heller, "The empty throne waits for the Messiah. If someone occupies this throne, we can be certain: this is perverted or false Messiah."[12] The ritual's tacit demand for a true and just political order testifies to the transformative potential within the life of the people nation, which Pope Francis acknowledges:

> People in every nation enhance the social dimension of their lives by acting as committed and responsible citizens, not as a mob swayed by the powers that be....Yet becoming a *people* demands something more. It is an ongoing process in which every new generation must take part: a slow and arduous effort calling for a desire for integration and a willingness to achieve this through the growth of a peaceful and multifaceted *cultura del encuentro* ("culture of encounter"). (*Evangelii Gaudium* 220)

Becoming a people, therefore, is the "slow and arduous" work of generations. Commitment to time rather than space is a commitment to process rather than looking for easy answers in the present. Francis draws attention to the sense of a proper time to make a right decision, whether existential, interpersonal, pastoral, social, or political. It clearly derives from the Ignatian tradition of discernment; specifically, the "Election" or moment of choice in the Second Week of the *Spiritual Exercises* as a moment that must be carefully prepared for, so that the retreatant deciding is in a state of balance and indifference before God.

For Francis, it holds out the possibility of mediating controversies — such as conflicting views on the theology of the family. When he writes that there is not always a need for a decisive intervention of the magisterium, we should remember that the word *decide* comes from the Latin for "to kill," that is, to eliminate one or more of the options. Francis's point (I think) is that some issues need to be given time. Not all pastoral contexts are the same, and differences need to be respected rather than flattened out by a premature judgment.

Here, we need only reflect on the essentially conflictive nature of many spatial metaphors. It is impossible for two people to share the same physical space, though they share the same time continuum. So if we are overconcerned with space, then we tend toward competition and separation rather than unity: we "take a stand," or we "adopt a position," we "form a camp," we "defend our corner." And according to the second principle, unity must take priority over conflict.

"Time's priority over space" is demonstrated in several biblical parables, above all Matthew's parable of the wheat and the tares (Matt 13:24–30). The instinct of the servant is to "clear the space," to remove the weeds that have adulterated it so that the field will be pure again. But the master, knowing this will merely destroy the wheat, orders that wheat and weeds should grow together until the harvest separation. And there are other parables where Jesus indicates that the solution to a problem is one of allowing *time*: the ungrateful servant who pleads, "Give me time and I will repay" (but then refuses to show the same mercy to the servant indebted to him!), and the unproductive tree, with the exasperated master who wants to cut it down — this time it is the servant who urges that it be given one more year.

THE THEO-POLITICS OF TIME

The priority of time over space is not just intended as a guiding principle for pastors and moral theologians. It is meant to hold good for all decision processes including those in the political realm. So what might be its implications for political theology?

The young people in Rio de Janiero were given the message that "time initiates processes, and space crystallizes them," giving a priority therefore to actions that "give birth to new historical dynamics."[13] Here is an echo, surely, of Hannah Arendt's argument—drawing on Augustine—for "natality," rather than mortality, as the defining root of our "human condition." Our "natal" status defines authentic self-disclosure, not a mere recoil from mortality, such as we find, for example, in Heidegger and other philosophers. We are born alone, and we do indeed die alone—but it is the first of these facts, not the second, that is decisive for human authenticity.[14] The fact that we are natal grounds Arendt's notion of political action.

Augustine offers further guidance on time's priority over space. When Augustine used the term *saeculum* (from which derives our word *secular*), he had in mind an age or epoch. The *saeculum* is the period during which the two cities, earthly and heavenly, are intermingled. They will coexist until the end-time. We are reminded of Matthew's parable of the wheat field, once again. However, in the modern age, we have come into the habit of regarding the *saeculum*, not as a period of time, but as a space. We now speak of the "secular sphere," "realm," etcetera. This is an unfortunate shift in our thinking that has impoverished Christian political self-understanding. It means, to paraphrase Francis, that we busy ourselves occupying spaces rather than initiating transformative processes.

This change of perspective is illustrated in the distinction between a map and an itinerary. The itinerary for a medieval pilgrimage, for example, described the journey as it seemed to someone actually undertaking it. In the modern age, in which space has been explored, colonized, regulated, mapped out, and so on, we are more likely to open out a map and to plan the same journey "from above."[15]

A map gives us some information, but it is not the same as physically making the pilgrimage. The danger is that we convince ourselves that we know the route—when all we have is a representation of it. To apply this to the theological method of Pope Francis: he is interested in an itinerary for life's pilgrimage rather than a map. He is concerned about the day-to-day, moment-to-moment experience of the journey rather than what that journey looks like when represented from above.

We will return to the implications of time's priority for Francis when we examine its development in other sections of *Amoris Laetitia*. First, however, an important conversation needs to be opened between what we have understood so far of Francis's theological method and what was propounded by Johann Baptist Metz in *Faith in History and Society*.[16] The title of Metz's "practical fundamental theology" is itself suggestive, as a parallel to Francis's own explicit "faith" in historical processes, on the one hand, and in *el pueblo*, the people nation as the vehicle of God's purposes, on the other.

J. B. METZ ON MESSIANIC TIME

In *Faith in History and Society*, Metz highlights the ambiguity of the project of secularization, which had been at the center of his earlier work. The problem is that modernity is now seen to be undermining and threatening the subject to which it gave birth. Its capability and potential have given way to a paralyzing weariness, the "second immaturity" implicit in so much postmodern thinking. Perhaps we do not really want to become Enlightenment "subjects" after all?

Metz associates this numbness with what he calls "timelessness," in a chapter titled "Hope as Immanent Expectation, or the Struggle for Lost Time." The new indolence has its own form of metaphysics, which Metz calls "the logic of evolution" (Thesis VIII).[17] According to this logic, time has been made indifferent—or rather we are talking about an experience of timelessness, on which everything is reconstructed. In this way, the emancipation of the modern subject is subverted: the *bourgeois* subject who remains is defined in terms of a shrunken or truncated notion of freedom, namely "freedom from suffering," an insulation or buffering from the suffering of others.

Capitalist modernity has evacuated sacred time. Holy seasons—sabbaths, jubilees etcetera, are necessary for the spirit of resistance to be nurtured and renewed—but these have been effaced by the frenzy of consumerism, as we are reminded in Walter Benjamin's fragment

"Capitalism as a Religion."[18] Metz's fifth thesis laments how "catastrophes are reported on the radio in between pieces of music" with the music continuing to play inexorably like the audible passage of time: "No one shouts 'stop it!' anymore...."[19] There is a reminder here of Walter Benjamin once again, and his "Angel of History," who longs to stay and make whole what has been smashed in the catastrophes of history—but his wings are caught in the unstoppable storm of progress, hurtling him backward into the future.[20]

Here is the importance of the "dangerous memory" of Jesus Christ. The new indolence that is creeping over society needs to be "interrupted." The sixth of Metz's theses declares simply, "The shortest definition of religion: interruption."[21] The "dangerous memory," acting as interruption, remembers not only what has succeeded, but what has been destroyed and lost (Thesis VII). The "buffered self" of the Enlightenment middle-class subject needs to be reconfigured as *the subject of suffering*, whose freedom consists in the freedom to enter into the suffering of others. Like Walter Benjamin, Metz stresses not the optimistic, evolutionary history of the victors, but the forgotten history of victims. History, in the light of the memory of Christ's passion and resurrection, must be reconsidered as a history of those who have suffered and died. By the same token, apocalyptic or "messianic" thinking is a rhetorical device against sleepiness. Apocalypse is a radical hope for the other, even for one's enemies, by a prayerful disposition that Metz names *Leiden an Gott*, a "suffering toward God."[22]

We shall ask later how this conception of two kinds of time—"evolutionary" and "messianic"—might be related to Pope Francis and his stress on the "priority of time over space." But we should note a paradox: both Walter Benjamin and Johann Baptist Metz each understand human flourishing, not in terms of the progressive forces of history, but in terms of putting a brake on those forces, of "interrupting" history, in order to "stay, awaken the dead, and make whole what has been smashed."[23]

"FRANCISCAN" THEMES: "SEEDS OF THE WORD" AND "GRADUALNESS"

Having introduced Metz into the conversation, I would like now to return to *Amoris Laetitia*, and to two themes that, in different ways, highlight the priority of time over space: "seeds of the word" and "gradualness." "Seeds of the Word" is the term used by the synod fathers to stress that the marriage relationship is a natural good, built into the created order, but one that points eschatologically, as it were, to a glorious fulfillment in the person of Christ. Just as a seed is oriented to the flower it will become, so "the order of redemption illuminates and fulfils that of creation" (*Amoris Laetitia* 77). Only in Christ do we come to know the deepest truth about human relationships. The idea is an ancient one. Justin Martyr spoke in the second century of the *logos spermatikos*, the "seed of the Word," to be found even in the hearts of unbelievers. This optimistic doctrine about the human propensity for God highlights, once again, the importance of the time the seed requires for its growth.

It is striking how Francis applies this analogy of "seeds of the word" to the reality of marriage. The very fact of starting a family—regardless of faith background or lack of it—is welcomed as a courageous, eschatological sign of truth and love: "Anyone who wants to bring into this world a family is…[making a] gesture aimed at overcoming evil…whatever the people, religion or region to which they belong!" (*Amoris Laetitia* 77).

Another element of Francis's strategy in *Amoris Laetitia*, and where once again the priority of time is evident, is the notion of "gradualness" in pastoral care (no. 8).[24] Francis cites Pope John Paul II as introducing the notion of the "law of gradualness," that the human being "knows, loves and accomplishes moral good by different stages of growth." This is not a relativization of the law itself, but a recognition that people are at different stages on their journey toward the ideal: "Each human being advances gradually with the progressive integration of the gifts of God and the demands of God's definitive and absolute love in his or her entire personal and social life" (no. 295). This journey toward truth will require "a process of accompaniment and discernment which guides the faithful to an awareness of their situation before God" (no. 300). In this process, the priest is there to form a conscience, not to replace it. Once again, the emphasis is on refraining from the moment of judgment or decision, to nurture a more authentic process or journey.

Marco Politi's biography *Pope Francis among the Wolves* gives an example of "the Bergoglio difference." The then archbishop of Buenos Aires counseled a priest who had decided to leave priestly ministry and live with a woman. Bergoglio agreed to start the paperwork to release him from the clerical state, but advised him not to have children for a year or two. When the relationship fell apart and the priest wanted to return to the priesthood, the archbishop agreed once again to initiate the paperwork on condition that the man live as a chaste layman for five years. "Today, they say, he is one of the most respected priests in the capital."[25]

CONVERSATION

None of this holds together easily. Pope Francis quotes Thomas Aquinas, that staying on the level of general principles is dangerous for the pastoral theologian because the situation may look very different on a more detailed level: "The more we descend to matters of detail, the more frequently we encounter defects" (*Amoris Laetitia* 304). This passage highlights once again how "time is greater than space," or at least, how a spatial way of thinking can be limiting or distorting. Only when we descend from above "into detail," that is, go on to the ground level, do important features of a situation become visible. It is the difference, once again, between following an itinerary and scrutinizing a beautifully produced map.

The notions "seeds of the Word" and "gradualness" call our attention to Francis's view of pastoral care as not simply about turning away from sin and regularizing lifestyle and so on, but as inseparable from the call to spiritual growth and holiness. This is of course reflected in the Jesuit self-description, that to be a Jesuit is "to know oneself a sinner who is called to be a companion of Jesus." As we have already noted, it is movingly rendered in Francis's own self-awareness, referencing to Matthew 9. He states as much in the interview with Antonio Spadero: "I am a sinner whom the Lord has looked upon….I am one who is looked upon by the Lord."[26]

His motto, *Miserando atque Eligendo* ("By having mercy and by choosing him"), stresses this identification of forgiveness and call. This also brings us to the scandal and resistance to Pope Francis's pastoral strategy. His rupturing of the customary link of "mercy" and "forgiveness" is for some people a dangerous confusion. It requires us to recast our understanding of pastoral care of the sinner as a process, not of judgment, but of discernment and accompaniment. It is no different in kind from the accompaniment of someone exploring a vocation or advancing in a holy life. All are recipients of "mercy" and "grace" in a way that centuries of careful distinction between *gracia sanans* and *elevans*, of justification and sanctification, look as if they are being eroded.

I have attempted in this essay to examine Pope Francis's distinctively Argentinian theological style in the light of some key themes of political theology as expressed above all by Johann Baptist Metz. While there are clearly exciting areas of convergence and compatibility, there are other aspects where mutual questioning seems to be called for. Francis's theology is of course no more "infallible" than that of John Paul II or of Benedict XVI. With respect to his predecessors, we can ask nevertheless if there is a real paradigm shift at work in Francis. While his predecessors still operated from and within a European matrix, the "Franciscan spring" has, surprisingly, brought theologies of the South (such as the theology of liberation) back into full focus. In the light of this "mutually critical discussion" between Francis and Metz, three areas of further questioning emerge.

First, Francis's apparently unqualified support for "time's priority over space" needs to be set against Metz's two kinds of time. Metz speaks of how "evolutionary time," which is effectively an empty timelessness, has resulted in a drowsy and fatalistic amnesia, because any possibility of redemption in history has been hollowed out. This needs to be countered by "messianic" or eschatological time, whereby the "dangerous memory" of Jesus Christ keeps alive a solidarity with victims and reawakens the possibility of transformation. It is, clearly, the second of these, the transformative potential of time, which Francis has in mind when he speaks of deep historical purposes. However, we should note that Metz speaks of redemptive time not as a continuous historical process, but as a "dangerous memory" that breaks into and that *interrupts*. Like Benjamin's "Angel of History," the Messiah seeks to put a brake on history, not to impel it faster forward.

A second area of questioning, from a Metzian point of view, would be the concern about political idolatry, the imperative that the Messiah's throne be kept empty until his return. There is no doubt that aspects of the *teología del pueblo* sound odd, and perhaps even disturbing, to European ears, in the light of the disastrous history of nationalism in the twentieth century. It is, one hopes, possible to disentangle this style from more problematic aspects of cultural and political Peronism,[27] but it is not clear, after this has been done, what remains of the almost mystical trust in "the people" as the site of God's revelation. What makes the collective of *el pueblo* more convincing than the Marxist version of the proletariat? It is worth noting that Pope John Paul had similarly strong convictions of the "destiny" of the Polish people and nation for the renewal of European Christianity, though Pope Francis does not go as far as to single out the Argentinian people for such a role.

A related point can be made with respect to the importance of popular culture and religiosity. There is no doubt that this insistence was, and remains, an important theological corrective: first, of the "elitist" forms of liberation theology with which Jorge Bergoglio had to contend in Argentina, which dismissed traditional popular devotions as reactionary; and more generally, of any overintellectualized theological approach that is ungrounded in a respect for the life and worship of the poor believer. When Pope Francis declares in *Evangelii Gaudium* that "a people continuously evangelizes itself" through its popular piety, he is drawing on similar affirmations by the Latin American Bishops at their conferences in Puebla (1979) and Apparecida (2007) (no. 122).[28] On the other hand, some of the expressions of this priority by advocates of the *teología del pueblo* can be strikingly uncritical. It is certainly possible to identify festivals and devotions (such as the Tinkunaco fiesta in La Rioja) where spiritual wisdom is embedded and transmitted through generations. But what about other religious practices that serve as counterexamples: of fatalism, superstition, or vindictive "groupthink"? Francis recognizes the vocation of *el pueblo* as a call to act as "committed and responsible citizens, not as a mob swayed by the powers that be" (*Evangelii Gaudium* 220). But what precisely leads them to go one way and not another? Once again, a Metzian "pessimism" about the fragility of the modern subject, and the potential for being overwhelmed by totalitarian social forces, may serve as an important corrective.

CONCLUDING REMARKS

It is interesting to note that the suggested lines of critique mentioned in this essay invite us to reopen a previous debate, namely the discussion around Metz and what he called the "eschatological pro-viso." In the late 1960s, Metz had insisted that any present political arrangement, no matter how benign, could not simply be equated with the kingdom of God. If we are to avoid a repetition of the disas-trous false messianic politics of the twentieth century, then Christians must insist that any political regime is nonidentical, or *noncontempo-raneous*, with God's future. The church is the guardian of the "escha-tological proviso," a "refusal to bless the state."[29] This concept is not without its difficulties and came in for criticism from the liberation theologian Juan Luis Segundo. It seems to leave us with a negative and even passive view of Christian action and involvement. Surely the Christian task is one of proclamation, not just denunciation? Are we not called to identify the signs of the kingdom in the here and now, in contemporary political systems or movements, however imperfect?[30]

For a liberationist such as Segundo, this weakness highlighted the difference between Latin American liberation theology, which was not afraid to name the kingdom as "among us in the here and now," and European theology, whose fear of political messianism effectively postponed the kingdom to the future. It would be good to revisit this discussion in the light of Pope Francis and his very strong sense of God's presence even in the concrete actuality of popular devotion and culture. Are these two approaches incompatible, or can they be mutu-ally corrective and supportive?

As we have seen, an appreciation of and trust in popular reli-gious devotion is one of the hallmarks of Pope Francis's style. I write this essay in Manila, where I have made the delightful discovery of a vivid and charming devotion, *San José Dormido*. Pope Francis referred enthusiastically to it during his visit to the Philippines in January 2015, when he addressed a gathering of families in Manila:

> I would like to tell you something very personal. I like Saint Joseph very much. He is a strong man of silence. On my desk I have a statue of Saint Joseph sleeping. While sleep-ing he looks after the Church. Yes, he can do it! We know that. When I have a problem or difficulty I write on a piece of paper and put it under the statue so he can dream about it. This means please pray to Saint Joseph for this problem.

Next, rising with Joseph and Mary. These precious moments of repose, of resting with the Lord in prayer are moments we might wish to prolong. But like Saint Joseph once we have heard God's voice we must rise from our slumber: we must get up and act. (Romans 13.11) Faith does not remove us from the world, but draws us more deeply into it.[31]

Francis had the statue brought from Bueno Aires in Argentina to Rome. On the way the head was broken off, so it has been repaired. It rests outside Room 201 of Casa Santa Marta in Rome, where, it has been observed, sometimes the prayer requests pile up because the Holy Father works hard, like St. Joseph. Soon after his election as Pope, Francis is alleged to have told one of his collaborators:

> You know, you must be patient with these carpenters: they tell you they'll have a piece of furniture finished in a couple of weeks and it ends up taking a month even. But they get the job done and they do it well! You just need to be patient.[32]

May the "sleeping St. Joseph" assist and guide us always!

NOTES

1. See Juan Carlos Scannone, "Pope Francis and the Theology of the People," *Theological Studies* 77, no. 1 (2016): 128. My thanks to Chris Knowles for his assistance with material on the *teología del pueblo*.

2. Antonio Spadaro, "A Big Open Heart to God: The Exclusive Interview with Pope Francis," *America* 209, no. 8 (September 30, 2015): 15–38.

3. See https://w2.vatican.va/content/francesco/en/apost_exhortations/documents/papa-francesco_esortazione-ap_20131124_evangelii-gaudium.html.

4. Pope Francis, *2013 World Youth Day Homily*, posted July 30, 2016, http://www.catholicherald.co.uk/news/2016/07/30/full-text-pope-franciss-address-at-world-youth-day-prayer-vigil/.

5. Ibid.

6. Gustavo Gutierrez, *A Theology of Liberation: History, Politics, and Salvation*, 15th anniv. ed., trans. Caridad Inda and John Eagleson (Maryknoll, NY: Orbis, 1988).

7. Pope Francis, *Amoris Laetitia: The Joy of Love. Apostolic Exhortation on Joy in the Family* (London: Incorporated Catholic Truth Society, 2016).

8. Spadaro, "A Big Heart Open to God," 24.

9. Juan Carlos Scannone, "Perspectivas Eclesiologicas de la 'Teología del Pueblo' en la Argentina," no. 1, accessed on December 23, 2015, http://mercaba.org/FICHAS/Teologia_latina/perspectivas_eclesiologicas.htm. Translations from this article are by M. Kirwan.

10. Ibid., 1.2.a.

11. Juan Carlos Scannone, "The Symbolic Witnessing of the *Tinkunaco* Rite: Prophecy, Politics, and Popular Latin American Wisdom," *Witnessing: Prophecy, Politics and Wisdom*, ed. Maria Clara Bingemer and Peter Casarella (Maryknoll, NY: Orbis, 2014), 122–29.

12. Agnes Heller, "Politik nach dem Tode Gottes," *Jahrbuch Politische Theologie*, vol. 2 (Münster: Lit Verlag, 1997), 68–87, at 87; cited in Jürgen Manemann, "The Permanence of the Theological-Political: Opportunities and Threats for Christianity in the Current Crisis of Democracy," *Concilium* 2005, no. 3 (2005): 48–58, at 56.

13. *2013 World Youth Day Homily.*

14. Hannah Arendt, *The Human Condition* (Chicago: University of Chicago Press, 1970 [1958]), 176–77. Arendt cites St. Augustine: "That there be a beginning, man was created before whom there was nobody." Augustine, *The City of God*, xii, 20.

15. See especially William T. Cavanaugh, "From One City to Two: Christian Reimagining of Political Space," *Political Theology* 7, no. 3 (2006): 46–48.

16. Johann Baptist Metz, *Faith in History and Society: Toward a Practical Fundamental Theology*, trans. J. Matthew Ashley (New York: Crossroad, 2007).

17. Ibid., 158.

18. Walter Benjamin, "Capitalism as Religion," in *Walter Benjamin: Selected Writings, Volume 1:1913–1926*, ed. Marcus Bullock and Michael W. Jennings (Cambridge, MA: Belknap Press of Harvard University Press, 1996), 288–91.

19. Metz, *Faith in History and Society*, 157.

20. Walter Benjamin, "Theses on the Philosophy of History," *Illuminations*, ed. Hannah Arendt, trans. Harry Zohn (New York: Schocken, 1968), 257–58.

21. Metz, *Faith in History and Society*, 158.

22. An article by Metz titled "Leiden an Gott" is translated as "suffering unto God" by J. Matthew Ashley. See J. B. Metz and J. M. Ashley, "Suffering unto God," *Critical Inquiry* 20, no. 4 (Summer 1994): 611–22.

23. Benjamin, *Illuminations*, 257.

24. "Accompanying, Discerning, and Integrating Weakness."

25. Marco Politi, *Pope Francis among the Wolves: The Inside Story of a Revolution*, trans. William McCuaig (New York: Columbia University Press, 2015), 4.

26. Spadaro, "A Big Heart Open to God," 16.

27. Peronism (*peronismo*) is the postwar Argentinian political movement associated with President Juan Domingo Perón (1895–1974) and his wife, Eva. It is widely regarded as a form of corporate or "right wing" socialism, even though it understands itself as a third position ideology, rejecting both capitalism and socialism. Though *peronist* politics has over time embraced a range of contradictory perspectives, the most obvious characteristic of the movement is a populist identification of working class interests with national identity.

28. See also *Puebla Document* (1979), no. 450, and *Aparecida Document* (2007), no. 264.

29. The term "eschatological proviso" refers to the insistence that no political system or regime in the present age can fully and correctly be identified with God's final kingdom; this kingdom is an act of divine power that comes to us from the future, so to speak. We must in principle "refuse to bless the state," a term taken from R. A. Markus's essay on Augustine: "Refusing to Bless the State: Prophetic Church and Secular State," *New Blackfriars* 70 (1989): 372–79.

30. For a survey of the difference of opinions between Metz and J. L. Segundo, see Michael Kirwan, "Learning to Say No: Does the Eschatological Reserve Have a Future?" *Political Theology* 7, no. 3 (2006): 393–409.

31. "Pope Francis's Message to Families at the MOA Arena, Manila," 9–10, accessed December 23, 2016, https://www.scribd.com/

document/253246153/Pope-Francis-in-the-Philippines-Speeches-and
-Homilies.

32. "Those Little Prayers Francis Slips under His St. Joseph
Statue," *La Stampa*, April, 30, 2014, http://www.lastampa.it/2014/
04/30/vaticaninsider/eng/the-vatican/those-little-prayers-francis-slips
-under-his-st-joseph-statue-RtS7Azmhb1udlQEzub40fP/pagina.html.

4

Mercy, Theology, and Spirituality

Responding to the Wounds of a Crucified World

J. Matthew Ashley

> *Jesus Christ is the face of the Father's mercy. These words might well sum up the mystery of the Christian faith.*
> —Pope Francis, *Misericordiae Vultus*[1]
>
> *Jesus' gaze fell first and foremost not on others' sins, but on others' suffering....And this is how Christianity began: as a community that remembered and told stories in following Jesus, the Jesus whose gaze fell first on the other's suffering.*
> —Johann Baptist Metz, *Memoria passionis*[2]

In thinking on the centrality of mercy to Pope Francis's vision for the church, the theologies of Jon Sobrino and of Johann Baptist Metz come inevitably to mind.[3] Nothing could seem more natural than to seek out the complementarity in vision of these diverse figures, each of whom, in different ways, centers his theological proposal on mercy and compassion. Limits of space do not permit rendering a three-way conversation, as valuable as that would be.[4] I attend here only to Pope Francis's advocacy of mercy as "Jesus' most important message"[5] and Metz's insistence on the primordiality of compassion for Christianity.

It does not take long to discover discordance in the ways that they articulate their respective contentions as to what lies at the heart of Christian discipleship. The principal one can already be gleaned from the quotes with which I began—a tension between mercy and compassion that will be the generative dyad for my reflections. For the Pope, "Mercy is divine and has to do with the judgment of sin."[6] He goes on to distinguish mercy from compassion, which "has a more human face. [Compassion] means to suffer with, to suffer together, to not remain indifferent to the pain and the suffering of others."[7] Metz, conversely, does not make a distinction between mercy and compassion, indeed he appears purposely to ignore the former.[8] In the German political theologian's thought, the fundamental stance to which this disposition refers is *not* first and foremost a response to sin and guilt, whether we are talking about God's compassion as revealed in Jesus, or in the compassion that must be central to Christian discipleship. Indeed, Metz is critical of the early church precisely for displacing the sensitivity to suffering with a focus on sin and guilt. This displacement results in what he calls a "soteriological enspellment" of Christianity that is at the root of the privatization of Christian faith and its corresponding loss of credibility in the modern world.[9] Would not Pope Francis, on Metz's view, run the danger of falling under the same indictment?

I argue in what follows not only that Francis avoids this danger, but also that he has something to contribute to Metz's theology by showing how a relative distinction between mercy (as more on the divine side) and compassion (on the human side) is well worth building into "the new political theology." This would be very much a friendly amendment, since, after all, Metz always characterizes the moves he makes in his theology as "correctives" to one-sided emphases in the theological tradition, which must be rethought and renavigated as the signs of the times change.[10]

This is more than just the adjudication of a prima facie disagreement between two theologians (and I do not hesitate to name Pope Francis as such). It can contribute to the ongoing attempt to find a relatively adequate solution to one of the more serious problems in Catholic theology since the Second Vatican Council. That Council, particularly the document *Gaudium et Spes,* grappled with how to understand the relationship between the world's history and what we do in it, and the history of salvation, which can be thought of as what God is doing to save us and the world. We can take Francis's understanding of the importance of mercy, which responds to human sin and guilt, to focus on the history of salvation. Metz, and his emphasis on compassion as the only appropriate response to the suffering that is so much a part of human history (what he calls the "histories of suffering") looks more at the world's history. Are they separate histories? Is there only hope for individual souls and their redemption, but not for our collective work of making the world's history more a history of flourishing and less a history of suffering and failure? Working out how mercy and compassion relate to one another can provide a helpful window into this problem.

I begin by tarrying a bit longer with statements made by Pope Francis on mercy and its relationship to compassion, on the one hand, and Metz on compassion, and the suffering to which it responds, on the other. Areas of overlap will emerge that trouble the overly sharp distinction with which I began. Moreover, what we will find in the process is that while both do relate mercy and compassion within different conceptual frames, this dyad ultimately finds its unity in a radical following of Christ best approached discursively through the language of Christian spirituality. For Metz, this spirituality is named as "an empathetic mysticism of opened eyes (c.f., Luke 10:25–37)," that is, a political mysticism of compassion.[11] For Pope Francis, the Jesuit, it is the spirituality worked out by Ignatius of Loyola in his *Spiritual Exercises.*[12] Some exploration of the latter will reveal an understanding of the relationship between the experience of God's mercy and the call to discipleship that will complete my argument for complementarity between the two theological visions.

MERCY AND COMPASSION: A HYPOSTATIC COMPLEMENTARITY

When asked about the relationship between mercy and compassion, Francis begins, as we saw earlier, by mapping them onto the distinction between the divine and the human: "Mercy is divine and has to do with the judgment of sin. Compassion has a more human face. It means to suffer with, to suffer together, to not remain indifferent to the pain and suffering of others."[13] He also emphasizes confession and the experience of forgiveness of sins mediated by the church's sacraments as the most fundamental loci for the event of mercy given and received.[14] But further reading complicates any attempt to make a clean distinction between mercy and compassion. He very frequently mentions them together. Considering God's presence in history as described in the Hebrew Bible, he writes that "the mercy of God is not an abstract idea, but a concrete reality with which he reveals his love as of that of a father or a mother, moved to the very depths, out of love for their child. It is hardly an exaggeration to say that this is a 'visceral' love. It gushes forth from the depths naturally, *full of tenderness and compassion, indulgence and mercy*" (*Misericordiae Vultus* 6, emphasis added).

Francis explores this relationship further by turning to Jesus Christ. "Jesus of Nazareth, by his words, his actions, and his entire person reveals the mercy of God" (*Misericordiae Vultus* 1). During this exploration, mercy and compassion are often, indeed usually, named together. "He had compassion for them, because they were like sheep without a shepherd" (Mark 6:34). In describing Jesus's response to the widow of Nain, he writes, "He had compassion for her" (Luke 7:13). "God loves us in this way, with compassion and mercy."[15] For Francis, mercy and compassion comingle the same way that the divinity and humanity do in Jesus Christ, following a logic of what is called the hypostatic union: never separate, but not to be conflated.[16] "The signs he works, especially in favor of sinners, the poor, the marginalized, the sick, and the suffering, are all meant to teach mercy. Everything in him speaks of mercy. Nothing is devoid of compassion" (*Misericordiae vultus* 8).

So too, then, for the church; "we are called to show mercy because mercy has first been shown to us" (*Misericordiae vultus* 9). And while this mercy will certainly manifest itself in forgiveness (sacramentally in the confessional, but not only there), it is just as strongly linked to compassion as it is in the life and work of Jesus of Nazareth: "The church's very credibility is seen in how she shows merciful and compassionate love" (no. 10). Mercy/compassion is rendered concrete in the spiritual and corporal works of mercy. It is also manifested in every action (both individual and corporate) that arises out of a set of fundamental dispositions that the pope connects with the action of love within the Trinity, defining God's merciful relationship to the world, and incarnate in the praxis of Jesus: patience; joyfulness; peace; an inclusive love that excludes no one, reaching out in particular to those on the margins; a love that builds bridges; a hospitality that makes all feel welcome, that forebears judging and condemning others (*Evangelii Gaudium* 112–14). In his address to the Jesuits at their 36th General Congregation, Francis describes mercy as a horizon or integrating principle for one's life as a whole: "Mercy is not an abstraction but a lifestyle consisting in concrete gestures rather than mere words: reaching out and touching others and institutionalizing the works of mercy."[17]

In conclusion, for Francis, there *is* a certain asymmetry that warrants attributing mercy first to God and giving it primacy. Mercy is the stance that an omnipotent God takes toward a weak, sinful humanity, loving us first. Indeed, it is precisely the marker of God's transcendence and omnipotence.[18] This justifies naming it distinctly. Yet mercy also marks an asymmetry that is preceded by a profound and empathetic love, and thus an asymmetry that overcomes itself, kenotically as it were, to become a solidaristic compassion (Phil 2:1–11).

For his part, as I already indicated, Metz concedes that his prioritization of responding to suffering (compassion) over responding to sin and guilt (mercy, forgiveness, reconciliation) is a corrective move. It is intended to correct a deeply rooted tendency in the church's theology and pastoral practice to focus so much on sin and the forgiveness of sin that we forget, overlook, or downplay (as "merely" physical and not spiritual) the suffering of the world, which requires compassion, and particularly requires compassion as a principle for Christian sociopolitical action. Yet he also vigorously resists the critical theorists with whom he has been in dialogue for the past six decades when they follow a broadly Marxist tendency to see in the latter a mere epiphenomenon of the former, in such a way that emancipation from suffering, earned through hard human work in history, can and should displace any notion of a merciful redemption from outside history.[19] Metz insists that the category of the history of suffering to which Christian faith and theology, indeed, any human aspiration for wholeness must attend, must be maximally broad, so that it includes the painful experience of sin and guilt, the experience of one's own failures and complicity in a history in which, as Walter Benjamin famously said, "There is no document of civilization which is not at the same time a document of barbarism."[20] This guilt and remorse threaten to paralyze us in our work of becoming and remaining together, "subjects in God's presence," by which Metz means mature women and men who take responsibility for their common history and for steering it toward a world in which flourishing is more the norm instead of meaningless suffering. As a means of dealing with this threatening dimension of human action in history, prayers of lament and contrition are political actions, since they empower continued action despite our failures and guilt. And they do this precisely by appealing to divine *mercy*.[21] Thus, on his own terms, Metz can at least work out a space for mercy in his broader insistence on compassion.

In Francis's mapping, the distinction between mercy and compassion is first articulated in terms of an asymmetry in our relationship to God, in which God always mercifully reaches out to us first in our failures and rejection of God.[22] Metz locates this transcendence differently: in his "untimely" advocacy of apocalyptic language and sensibility in theology.[23] God is the Lord of history, as the apocalyptic traditions insist, but on Metz's view, we are threatened today with an understanding of history that knows *no* lordship, divine or human, but unfolds relentlessly and pitilessly under the aegis of the logic of "evolution":

> At any rate: the modern world, with its scientific-technological civilization, is not simply a "rational universe." Its myth is evolution. The tacit interest behind its rationality is the fiction of time as an empty, surprise-free continuum, in which everything and everyone is gracelessly encompassed. The social symptoms of this are hard to miss: on the one hand, rampant apathy, on the other, mindless hatred; here fatalism, there fanaticism.[24]

People no longer expect anything new and surprising in history, only more of the same, and "the same" has become increasingly hostile to more and more of the earth's population (indeed, for the whole biosphere). This "evolutionary" sense for time and history feeds apathy and indifference, a hopelessness regarding the future that makes it unbearable to contemplate the suffering of the present and past. This comes together in a perfect storm with the compulsion to repress our sense of guilt and complicity in creating that present to result in a further paralysis of effective social and political action for the good of the whole human race and the whole planet.

This crisis of indifference and apathy has become a central theme of Francis's papacy as well:

> Some people continue to defend trickle-down theories which assume that economic growth, encouraged by a free market, will inevitably succeed in bringing about greater justice and inclusiveness in the world....To sustain a life-style which excludes others, or to sustain enthusiasm for that selfish ideal, a globalization of indifference has developed. Almost without being aware of it, we end up being incapable of feeling compassion at the outcry of the poor, weeping for other people's pain, and feeling a need to help them, as though all of this were someone else's responsibility and not our own. (*Evangelii Gaudium* 54; cf. *Misericordiae Vultus* 15)

Metz's insistence on the importance of Christianity's and Judaism's apocalyptic traditions is framed by this globalization of indifference. For the apocalyptic traditions, God's omnipotence is named in terms of God's capacity to interrupt history and its seemingly inexorable production of "more of the same." Christians enact and continue these traditions, not, Metz maintains, by trying to calculate "the day and the hour," or by indulging in violent fantasies about the end, but rather by their refusal to confine what they hope for within the bounds of what "any reasonable person" considers possible under the allegedly ironclad laws of economic and political development. And they act out of that hope: "Discipleship in imminent expectation: this is the apocalyptic consciousness that does not cause suffering, but shoulders it—defying apathy as well as hatred."[25] This sense for time, and for God's omnipotent "bounding" of time and history, is what makes a radical following of Christ possible: "The Christian idea of discipleship and the apocalyptic idea of imminent expectation absolutely belong together. It would not be possible to live a radical following of Jesus—that is, one that gets at the roots—'if the time were not shortened.' Jesus's call, 'Follow me!' cannot be separated from Christians' call, 'Come Lord Jesus!'"[26]

In sum, Pope Francis distinguishes mercy and compassion only to link them again when considering them in the context of salvation as a whole, and of the (hi)story of Jesus of Nazareth in particular. If mercy marks an asymmetry in our relationship to God, the omnipotent and Holy One, this mercy immediately inclines to dwell with us in compassion, because both mercy and compassion are rooted in a deeper "visceral" love of God for the world. Metz, for his part, emphasizes compassion almost to the point of eliding mercy because of his concern about the impact of focusing exclusively and relentlessly on sin, which Metz names the "hamartological overburdening of humanity,"[27] but only "almost." In considering the suffering on which Jesus's gaze first falls, he includes the suffering that comes from the guilt and remorse that threaten to paralyze us in our work of becoming and remaining, together, "subjects in God's presence." A *merciful* response by God is thus factored into the broader framework of compassion.

Metz also recognizes an asymmetry in our relationship to God, not referring to a prevenient divine mercy, but in reference to God's sovereign transcendence of history. For Metz, God is always the God beyond history, to whom history and time belong, and who can be called hopefully—even defiantly—to account for the suffering and sin in history, expecting a response. This hopeful stance toward God also informs the Christian's action in history, providing her or him a radical hope for committed action, even when it seems otherwise "unreasonable." Thus, Metz's theology is not allergic to the asymmetry between us and God that could be expressed by using the language of mercy, but he will do justice to this asymmetry using the language of apocalypticism. While Francis, then, emphasizes mercy, it is in a "hypostatic union" with compassion, and while Metz prioritizes compassion—our first response must be to the other's suffering rather than his or her sin—he does not exclude the suffering entailed by guilt and sin, and, consequently, the mercy and forgiveness that constitutes the divine response.

MISERANDO ATQUE ELIGENDO: MERCY, COMPASSION, AND CHRISTIAN DISCIPLESHIP

An important clue has emerged for finding a further coordination of the different ways that Francis and Metz speak about mercy and compassion, and set priorities between them: Christian discipleship and the language of Christian spirituality that is connected with it. Earlier I argued that Metz's insistence on apocalyptic ways of thinking and talking about God is in service to radical discipleship, and in the last fifteen years, he has come increasingly to focus on the foundational role, both for discipleship and a fortiori for theology, of a particular spirituality: "a mysticism of open eyes," open, that is, to the suffering of others in the world.[28] For his part, Pope Francis has criticized theologians when they wall themselves off in the analysis of theological concepts, opposing life in all its messiness with the supposed purity of concepts, so that "life has no room for reflection and reflection finds no room for life."[29] His own difference in style in this regard, vis-à-vis his two predecessors in the See of Rome, is amply evident from the encyclicals and apostolic exhortations that have emerged during the first four years of his pontificate. Most striking is his frequent deployment of the language and traditions of Christian spirituality—*Laudato Si'* comes to mind. While Francis of Assisi finds pride of place there, it is beyond doubt that it is Ignatian spirituality that most decisively shapes the Pope's thought, and so proffers another avenue into understanding how he relates mercy and compassion.

I pursue this avenue by considering a retreat that then Cardinal Bergoglio gave to the bishops of Spain in 2006. It is a promising text because in it he focuses on mercy, the call to Christian mission on behalf of others, and on "combative hope."[30] I suggest that a careful reading of how Francis presents the grace of mercy, as it is made available through the spirituality of Ignatius's *Exercises*, discloses a deeper internal connection with compassionate action for others and the hope connected with both. This will provide an additional point of correlation with Metz's approach.

In the *Spiritual Exercises*, the experience of mercy is the expected—or, perhaps better, prayed and hoped for—grace of the so-called First Week, in which the retreatant reflects on the destructive, death-dealing power of sin, a power with which he or she has been complicit. In Ignatius's spiritual logic of discipleship, the gratitude that this experience will unleash provides the proper context for making a choice of a particular way of following Jesus, which occurs in the Second Week.[31] In the opening meditation that he proposes to the Spanish bishops for the First Week, in a section titled "The One Who Reprimands and Pardons Us," Francis innovatively ties these moments—the experience of mercy and the choice of a specific form of following Jesus—very tightly together.

The Scripture passage he proposes is what he calls the first confession of Peter in Luke 5:1–11.[32] The context is already one of evangelization. Jesus has been teaching from Peter's boat. Then he has the disciples put out into deep waters and astounds them, indeed frightens them, with the miraculous catch of fish. Peter falls to his knees and confesses himself a sinner, and Jesus gives an unexpected response. It is *not* one of forgiveness, at least directly. Francis's parsing of this passage is worth quoting in full:

> The Lord accepts his *"Depart from me, Lord, for I am a sinful man"* (Luke 5:8) but he reorients it with his *"Do not be afraid; from now on you will be catching men"* (Luke 5:10). From that moment on, Simon Peter never separates these two dimensions of his life: he will also confess that he is a sinful man and a fisher of men. His sins will not prevent him from accomplishing the mission he has received (and he will never become an isolated sinner enclosed within his own sinfulness). His mission will not allow him to hide his sin, concealed behind a pharisaical mask.[33]

In terms of the logic of the *Spiritual Exercises* just mentioned, what Francis does with this passage is to link, indissolubly, the First Week and its experience of mercy, and the Second Week, with its focus on mission and finding one's own way of being a follower of Christ. This linking provides the latticework for a life of "contemplation in action," moved by the neediness of the world wherever it is perceived, but particularly "on the margins."[34] To be sure, God's mercy is still the premise and starting point correlative to the experience of sin, guilt, and failure, but the experience of mercy is not complete without experiencing the invitation to mission. "True conversion always entails an apostolic dimension! It always means to stop focusing on one's 'own interests' and to start looking after the 'interests of Christ Jesus.'"[35] The forgiveness of Peter's sin is not explicitly mentioned, even though Jesus does not deny Peter's "confession." But forgiveness transpires as an internal moment to the call to follow Jesus. Mercy and forgiveness are presented as something very far from a patronizing condescension that confirms the recipient in his or her subordinate status. Rather, mercy forgives by ennobling, pardons by calling to join in the work of healing the world's wounds.[36]

Metz's concern that a focus on sin, guilt, and forgiveness blinds the "mysticism of open eyes," which looks first on the suffering of the other rather than on guilt, is more than met. Far from distracting one or focusing one's attention on one's own private sinfulness before God ("he will never become an isolated sinner enclosed within his own sinfulness"), *this* way of framing the experience of mercy is precisely an impetus toward "combative" action on behalf of others. What is more, acting in a demanding history does not assume or require that we be perfect and that we hide our failures from others or from ourselves. This transformative and empowering experience of mercy is one that Pope Francis has himself lived, and has, indeed, found expression in his episcopal (and now papal) motto: "*Miserando atque eligendo,*" having mercy and choosing. Having mercy *by* choosing, perhaps.

CONCLUSION

I have argued that while Francis prioritizes mercy and forgiveness of sin, it is never to the exclusion of compassion for all kinds of suffering, as he often mentions them together, tied in a kind of hypostatic union. Metz insists on making room for the experience of mercy, even if he refuses to prioritize it. Both articulate their positions in the context of the danger posed by a growing sociocultural climate of indifference to suffering, and both find the most potent resources for fighting back to lie not in conceptual theological arguments (including those about the relationship between mercy and compassion), but rather in a lived following of Jesus that encompasses both mercy and compassion, a radical discipleship most clearly articulated in Christianity's spiritual traditions.

Metz's political theology has much to gain from considering Francis's proposal. With all its power to elicit and sustain radical historico-political hope and action, apocalypticism's God who "bounds history" as its saving interruption, the God "who is in coming," can leave us longing for a God who is with us *now*, in our frailty and in the seeming paltriness of what our efforts can achieve. Besides needing the courage and utopian imagination to think of a future that is radically more than "more of the same," we also need the courage to act in the painful awareness that we have fallen short in the past, and will continue to fall short of that for which a graced imagination can inspire us to hope. The experience of mercy that Francis limns using Ignatius's *Spiritual Exercises* presents to us a relationship to Christ that nourishes this kind of courage, and in its own way, elicits a combative hope. Far from desensitizing us to the suffering we see around us, it empowers us to respond in our frailty, limitations, and yes, sinfulness, knowing that we will fall short of attaining that for which we hope and long with our apocalyptically provoked imaginations. However, Metz's emphasis on apocalypticism's hope for a radically different future can strengthen the combative hope for which Francis advocates, especially when it comes to the globalized and now seemingly irresistible and irreformable economic and political structures of neoliberal capitalism.

The differences remain. Perhaps the most basic is the difference between an eschatological sense for God's agency in history, in which God works through the weak and frail agencies of inner mundane actors to bring about God's designs, and the apocalyptic sense of God interrupting the course of things when they appear most hopeless to bring about something utterly new and unexpected, for which no inner mundane causal sequence provides adequate explanation.[37] The need for both kinds of discourse and their inner unity, despite being irreducible to one another, is a function of God's presence to history, which is ultimately a mystery to be embraced and incarnated anew in one's own life before being conceptually probed. Both Pope Francis and Johann Baptist Metz provide insightful tools for that probing, but for both, the end goal is the same:

> I see the church as a field hospital after battle. It is useless to ask a seriously injured person if he has high cholesterol and about the level of his blood sugars! You have to heal his wounds. Then we can talk about everything else. Heal the wounds, heal the wounds....And you have to start from the ground up.[38]

NOTES

1. Pope Francis, *Misericordiae Vultus: Bull of Indiction of the Extraordinary Jubilee of Mercy*, no. 1; quoted here from a book in

which it is included as an appendix: Pope Francis, *The Name of God Is Mercy: A Conversation with Andrea Tornielli*, trans. Oonagh Stranksy (New York: Random House, 2016), 105.

2. Johann Baptist Metz, im Zusammenarbeit mit Johann Reikerstorfer, *Memoria passionis: Ein provozierendes Gedächtnis in pluralistischer Gescellschaft* (Freiburg: Herder, 2006), 163–64. Translation mine.

3. On Jon Sobrino, see, inter alia, *The Principle of Mercy: Taking the Crucified People from the Cross* (Maryknoll, NY: Orbis Books, 1994). There is hardly a book or essay by Metz published after 1990 that does not feature the centrality of compassion for Christian faith, practice, and theology.

4. A correlation with Sobrino's thought would be particularly instructive for gaining greater clarity on Jorge Mario Bergoglio's evolving stance toward "liberation theology."

5. Francis, *The Name of God Is Mercy*, 5.

6. Ibid., 91.

7. Ibid.

8. He hardly ever uses the closest German translation for mercy, *Barmherzigkeit*. *Compassion* (and he prefers to use it as a loanword from English) is the omnicompetent term for how God responds to the human condition, one which we are called to imitate as disciples.

9. See, e.g., Johann Baptist Metz, "Theology and Theodicy," in *A Passion for God: The Mystical-Political Dimension of Christianity*, with a foreword by the author, trans. and ed., with intro. by J. Matthew Ashley, (Mahwah, NJ: Paulist Press, 1998), 62–63; *Memoria passionis*, 165, 179–84.

10. See Johann Baptist Metz, *Faith in History and Society: Toward a Practical Fundamental Theology*, ed. and trans. (with a study guide) J. Matthew Ashley (New York: Crossroad Publishing, 2007), 30, 253n16.

11. Metz, "1492—through the eyes of a European Theologian," 15.

12. For an extended interpretation of the *Spiritual Exercises* by Francis, see the texts of talks that he gave to bishops of Spain on retreat in 2008: *In Him Alone Is Our Hope: Spiritual Exercises Given to His Brother Bishops in the Manner of St. Ignatius of Loyola* (New York: Magnificat, 2013).

13. Francis, *The Name of God Is Mercy*, 91, emphasis added. This is a definition of compassion with which Metz would be in complete agreement.

14. Ibid., 21–35.

15. Francis, *The Name of God Is Mercy*, 92.

16. Ever since the Council of Chalcedon in 451 CE, the term *hypostatic union* has been used to indicate how the human and divine natures are found in Jesus Christ in one person, or hypostasis (from the Greek). Jesus's divinity and humanity cannot be divided out into different parts of his total person; nor is he a kind of mixture, or "third thing" besides being human and divine. The precise way it is stated in the Creed is this: "One and the same Christ, Son, Lord, Only-begotten, to be acknowledged in two natures, *inconfusedly, unchangeably, indivisibly, inseparably*; the distinction of natures being by no means taken away by the union, but rather the property of each nature being preserved, and concurring in one Person and one Subsistence," accessed December 17, 2016, https://www.ccel.org/ccel/schaff/creeds2.iv.i.iii.html. My point here is that Francis is suggesting that we think of mercy, with its more divine dimension, and compassion, as a more human response to the world, in the same way, because that is how they are found in Jesus. Mercy is not somehow lessened by its union with compassion, and vice versa. Both are perfect in their union with the other. To be sure, this is an abstract statement of a reality that must be incarnated anew in each person's life, which, as we shall see, Francis emphasizes as well.

17. "Address of His Holiness Pope Francis to the 36th General Congregation of the Society of Jesus," October 24, 2016, https://w2.vatican.va/content/francesco/en/speeches/2016/october/documents/papa-francesco_20161024_visita-compagnia-gesu.html.

18. He cites Thomas Aquinas: "'It is proper to God to exercise mercy, and he manifests his mercy particularly in this way.' Saint Thomas Aquinas's words show that God's mercy, rather than a sign of weakness, is the mark of his omnipotence" (*Misericordiae Vultus*, §6, citing the *Summa Theologiae*, II–II, q. 30, a. 4).

19. See "Redemption and Emancipation," in *Faith in History and Society*, 114–27; also see *A Passion for God*, 34–39; "Vergebung der Sünden," *Stimmen der Zeit* 195, no. 2 (February 1977): 119–28.

20. Walter Benjamin, "Theses on the Philosophy of History," in *Illuminations*, ed. with intro. Hannah Arendt, trans. Harry Zohn (New York: Schocken, 1968), 6.

21. See Johann Baptist Metz, "The Courage to Pray," in *Love's Strategy: The Political Theology of Johann Baptist Metz*, ed. John Downey (Harrisburg, PA: Trinity Press International, 1999), 157–66. "When faced with the consequences of our own actions, particularly as the movers of our common history, what alternative is there to despair *but the plea for forgiveness* and, according to the messianic light of hope, additional pleas precisely for those destroyed" (161–62, emphasis added). Here Metz, the German theologian, is thinking of the most disastrous consequence of his own history: the Holocaust.

22. "God is first; God is always first and makes the first move. God is a bit like the almond flower of your Sicily, Antonio, which always blooms first." Pope Francis and Antonio Spadaro, *A Big Heart Open to God: A Conversation with Pope Francis* (New York: Harper One, 2013), 49.

23. He argues this in a very condensed way in "Hope as Imminent Expectation—or, the Struggle for Lost Time," in *Faith in History and Society*, 156–65. See also "Theology versus Polymythicism: A Short Apology for Biblical Monotheism," in *A Passion for God*, 72–91.

24. Metz, *Faith in History and Society*, 159.

25. Ibid., 163.

26. Ibid.

27. See Metz, "Theology and Theodicy," 36.

28. For an extended argument regarding the foundational place of discipleship for Christian theology, see Johann Baptist Metz, *Followers of Christ: The Religious Life and the Church*, trans. Thomas Linton (Mahwah, NJ: Paulist Press, 1978). For his recent insistence on the mysticism of open eyes, see *Mystik der offenen Augen: Wenn Spiritualität aufbricht*, ed. Johann Reikerstorfer (Freiburg im Breisgau: Herder, 2011).

29. See "Videomensaje del Santo Padre Francisco al Congreso Internacional de Teología organizado por la Pontificia Universidad Católica Argentina," accessed October 9, 2016, https://w2.vatican.va/content/francesco/es/messages/pont-messages/2015/documents/papa-francesco_20150903_videomessaggio-teologia-buenos-aires.html. My translation, based on an English translation from Zenit: "Pope's Video Message to Theology Conference in Argentina," accessed June

11, 2017, https://zenit.org/articles/pope-s-video-message-to-theology-conference-in-argentina/.

30. While, as we shall see, the experience of mercy is crucial to the retreat he wants to lead them through, Francis begins by exhorting the bishops to pray for "the grace of a combative hope." See Francis, *In Him Alone Is Our Hope*, 10.

31. Indeed, it is *only* context Ignatius will allow. If the retreatant did not receive the grace of the First Week, Ignatius insisted that the retreatant not continue to "the election" in the Second Week.

32. Francis, *In Him Alone Is Our Hope*, 29–30.

33. Ibid., 30.

34. See "Address of His Holiness Pope Francis to the 36th General Congregation of the Society of Jesus."

35. Ibid.

36. One might say that this mirrors the classical Catholic position on grace and sin: grace heals by elevating. Thus, Christ forgives by calling.

37. Here the contrast between Metz and Francis aligns with that between Metz and his teacher, Karl Rahner, who disagreed precisely on the importance and possibility of using apocalyptic language today in Christian theology. For a discussion of the latter contrast, which might shed light on the former, see J. Matthew Ashley, *Interruptions: Mysticism, Politics and Theology in the Work of Johann Baptist Metz* (Notre Dame, IN: University of Notre Dame Press, 1998), 169–204.

38. Francis and Spadaro, *A Big Heart Open to God*, 30–31.

5

Hope and the Liberating Power of Mercy

Steve Ostovich

"Always be ready to make your defense to anyone who demands from you an accounting for the hope that is in you" (1 Pet 3:15b). This is the task of any fundamental theology, according to Johann Baptist Metz, and a challenge he has sought to meet in framing his new political theology as a fundamental theology. Our first concern here is to describe this hope with a particular focus on its temporal signature and consequent radical character. The argument that follows will be that mercy makes this hope reasonable and is the necessary concrete condition for hope. To do this we will look at Hannah Arendt's delineation of the human condition: we are plural beings capable of natality, that is, freedom as the capacity to birth the new. Given the world in which we live, our hope for justice and love is a hope for something new.

We will also see that for Arendt, this human condition is frail, because as plural beings we are enmeshed in a web of human relationships that affect us, and that, in acting, we affect but which we cannot control. We risk becoming ensnared in the lines of consequences of our actions and the actions of others to whom we are connected. For Arendt, the key to remaining free in this condition is forgiveness, and it is forgiveness that allows us to hope for the new, including justice and love. We will complete the argument by turning to mercy as a way of living that moves us beyond the act of forgiveness. There are limits to forgiveness for Arendt that we will examine below in the forensic context of punishment. Mercy moves us beyond these limits to a place where hope can give meaning to our acting for justice and in love.

HOPE

The content of our hope is what makes Metz's theology political: our hope is in the gospel promise of the kingdom of God as a community characterized by the political virtues of justice and love, which means no one can be saved alone. Hope here is not the same as optimism or a generally positive attitude toward the future, and it is not about our interior lives or feelings. Rather, hope is our critical principle for living and acting in the world: hope is the reason of political action.[1]

The temporal index of this hope is both surprising and significant. In principle, it seems possible to hope only for the future; after all, the past already has been determined and only the future seems open to shaping. Moreover, the specific hope we are examining here is for an *eschatological* community of justice—a community that has been promised justice, but in which justice clearly has not yet arrived. And yet believing our hope is only about that future fundamentally misunderstands the meaning of *eschaton*. The eschaton is not a *telos* of history or history's goal, or the aim of a linear process. The eschaton is the interruption of the flow of time. And so in apocalyptic literature, alongside the revelation of God's plan as an encouragement to believers to continue living according to the covenant despite being persecuted for doing so, one finds repeated admonitions that no one knows exactly when the end of this evil age will occur. It will come "like a thief in the night" (1 Thess 5:2). Time does not flow smoothly forward, and our hope is not in progress toward a goal. Indeed, our experience should teach us that faith in progress when it comes to justice is not warranted. While there have been instances of progress toward justice for some groups, one need only look at the twentieth century to undermine any confidence that we will progress to the community of God's love. Instead, we are called on to live believing any moment might be, in the words of Walter Benjamin (a thinker who has influenced Metz profoundly), "the small gateway in time through which the Messiah might enter."[2] Or, to put it in Metz's terms, "The shortest definition of religion: interruption."[3]

Understanding time as interruptive and eschatological, and not just simply as flowing progressively, reveals something startling about our hope: it is not just for the future but for the past as well, so our hope for justice includes justice for the dead. This is what Metz means by anamnestic solidarity, or "solidarity backward," with the past victims of injustice. Solidarity becomes critical in "anamnestic reason," the reason that remembers and is guided by the universal principle of suffering as its key critical category. This becomes practical through the "dangerous memories" of suffering that undermine the plausibility structures of what we accept as necessary and given. Such a dangerous memory is at the heart of the liturgical life of Christians as they celebrate the Eucharist as a ritual of promise through remembrance of the suffering, death, and resurrection of Jesus. Living this promise means our actions should reveal our hope, a hope whose eschatological disruptiveness takes the form of what Metz early on labeled the "eschatological proviso": any given social order is provisional and must be criticized and changed as it falls short of the promised community of justice and love.

This is what it means for hope to be a critical principle: our hope is revealed in our actions and is evident in our willingness to continue to work for justice and in the cause of love despite our frustrations and disappointments. Any successes we may have in the struggle to make our world a better place are at best only momentary and soon disappear. Hope makes our struggle reasonable even without success. As we are reminded by Paul, we are called to live *hos me*, "as not," a call neither to abandon this world nor to pretend we will succeed in making it into God's reign of justice and love. It is an invitation to question the plausibility structures of our age and to live and act according to God's eschatological promise.[4]

Mercy makes our hope possible. Pope Francis reminds us of this in *Misericordiae Vultus* when he writes, "Mercy is the force that reawakens us to new life and instils in us the courage to look to the future with hope" (no. 10).[5] To put this most strongly, mercy is the condition of possibility for hope, and not in an abstract or transcendental sense but concretely and practically. Mercy is what makes living in hope possible as well as reasonable.[6] Demonstrating why this is the case and what it means for our living mercifully and in hope is the point of the rest of this essay. To do so, we turn to the work of Hannah Arendt, particularly *The Human Condition*, where Arendt writes about mercy and forgiveness as liberating us for hope.

THE HUMAN CONDITION AND NATALITY

Hannah Arendt (1906–75) was a German-born Jew who fled the Third Reich in 1933 and, after experiencing episodes of internment and other forms of persecution, eventually arrived in the United States. Here she became a public intellectual and held academic appointments at several universities. *The Human Condition* could be called one of her more philosophical works were it not for the fact that she disdained being called a philosopher and thought of herself as a political theorist. The title of the work itself is an indication of her point in this book: Arendt is interested in the human condition, not human nature. In other words, she is not interested in doing traditional philosophical anthropology, but prefers to follow Augustine, for whom the important question to ask ourselves is "*Who* am I?" rather than "*What* am I?" For Augustine, only God as our Creator can seriously ask the latter question, but this is not Arendt's concern. For her, the issue is simply that "the human condition is not the same as human nature."[7] And this condition is plural: "we are all the same, that is, human, in such a way that nobody is ever the same as anyone else who ever lived, lives, or will live."[8] This is another reason to claim the correct question to ask ourselves is "who," not "what," we are.

Arendt draws on Augustine again to describe what it means for a plural being to be free. She defines freedom as *natality*, a word she coins to name the human capacity to do something new and unexpected and to be a beginning in time. Like Augustine in the *City of God* (XII, 20), Arendt claims that this capacity to birth the new first appeared in reality with us: "With the creation of man, the principle of beginning came into the world itself, which, of course, is only another way of saying that the principle of freedom was created when man was created but not before."[9] In using the word *natality*, Arendt emphasizes the connection between freedom and giving birth—humans give birth to the new—and the way in which the birth of every child represents a new beginning, something new coming into the world. It is only this capacity for birthing the new that "can bestow upon human affairs faith and hope," and "it is this faith in and hope for the world that found perhaps its most glorious and most succinct expression in the few words with which the Gospels announced their 'glad tidings': 'A child has been born unto us.'"[10] Our freedom, that is, our capacity for natality or giving birth to the new, enables our hope.

Natality offers a radically different model for freedom than our usual understanding of freedom in terms of the will. Arendt points this out repeatedly and claims this difference to be one of the strengths of freedom as natality. The capacity to do something new shifts our view toward the conditions under which one acts and away from the interiority of the agent. We thereby can step away from the unending and unfruitful discussion of the philosophical conundrums around determining how the will operates as free, especially in relation to reason. Natality also helps us resist the temptation to physiological or psychological reductionism as a way to deal with the problem of understanding the will. Perhaps its greatest strength is how natality helps us recover the meaning of politics that is absent from our current lives together. That politics has lost its meaning for us is obvious in our empty discourse about what we think is the place of politics in our lives in relation to our freedom. For the most part, we desire to be free *from* politics. The cost of this attitude is paid daily by those who suffer because we are unable to respond to suffering politically, an inability based on our fundamental misunderstanding of the meaning of politics. As Arendt states most directly, "The meaning of politics is freedom."[11]

Explaining why this is the case also exposes the "weak flank" of natality—freedom is not a matter of control or even predictability, despite what we believe based on our usual model of freedom as imposition of our will. Natality reminds us of the relation of action and plurality, and the fact that action takes place in the space between us—the space of politics. Arendt takes us back to the ancient Greek relation of *archein*, beginning something new, and *prattein*, seeing it through to completion.[12] My freedom consists in starting something new, but I depend on others to further along what I have started. She relates this issue to the arts: artists are models of natality in their creativity, but while the plastic artist leaves behind the artwork that endures, in acting we are more like the performing artist whose "work" ends with the performance and who depends on an audience for that work to have an afterlife.[13]

Natality exposes the frailty of action in a further way as well. I am not the only free being. You are free, too, and your actions can surprise me in a manner I cannot predict. I must be ready to respond to your freedom without trying to control you. This is because Arendt recognizes as a condition of freedom that my freedom depends on the freedom of others. We know this from our experience in relationships: in being close to another person, I am aware of my vulnerability, and I am tempted to respond by trying to control their reactions to me, only to find that by so doing I have damaged the relationship, sometimes beyond repair. I depend on others to be free if I am to be free, and freedom means letting go of the controlling impulse that would destroy freedom.[14]

FORGIVENESS

When I act, I act into what Arendt calls "the 'web' of human relationships."[15] The image of the web is meant both to help us understand the interconnectedness of plural beings and to trace the consequences of that interconnectedness. When I act, I start something and set a strand of the web vibrating; but I do not know all the connections of that strand, so I can't be certain about the outcome of my action. This extends even to ourselves: "Although everybody started his life by inserting himself into the human world through action and speech, nobody is the author or producer of his own life story."[16] And at the same time, I realize that my actions are irreversible, that once I have set a vibration loose on the web, I cannot call it back. I am responsible but without control. Life can be so uncertain.

Our usual response to this uncertainty is to try to gain greater control, but this would destroy freedom as natality. Instead of control, Arendt offers our capacities to *promise* and to *forgive* as responses to the uncertainty that results from living in a web of human relationships. Promises are like "isolated islands of certainty in an ocean of uncertainty."[17] Promises are not guarantees, but they allow us to orient ourselves as we navigate through the web of relationships and the consequences we have set loose in our natality. Arendt offers Abraham as a model of someone who responded to the uncertainty of God's call by formalizing promises through covenants, a topic to which we will return later.[18]

Forgiveness interests us more here, in part because Arendt does what we all often do, which is to use *forgiveness* and *mercy* interchangeably. Her practice is to write more about forgiveness, but in doing so, she also mentions concepts like the "Lord of Mercy." This loose equivalency of forgiveness and mercy is questioned in several of the essays in this volume, and it will be called into question in the discussion of mercy below. But what Arendt writes about forgiveness and its liberating power applies to mercy as well.

Acting into the web of human relationships sets off a chain of reactions, some that we anticipate but others that surprise or even dismay us—if we even know about them. How, then, can we escape being trapped in the web? How can action be free? This is where understanding freedom as natality becomes effective. The way to avoid being trapped by action is to do something unpredictable and give birth to the new: we forgive. "Forgiving, in other words, is the only reaction which does not merely re-act but acts anew and unexpectedly, unconditioned by the act which provoked it and therefore freeing from its consequences both the one who forgives and the one who is forgiven."[19] Forgiveness is not a matter of forgetting the past; it rather is responding to the past in a new and creative way. Forgiveness interrupts the chain of events set in motion by action and tries to move in a new direction in an act of natality.

Arendt's model for forgiveness is also biblical: Jesus of Nazareth. For Arendt, the heart of the gospel is forgiveness. She locates this not in the religious teaching of Jesus or in the religious teachings of Christianity about Jesus, but in what she takes to be the experience of Jesus among his small group of followers she reads in the gospel stories. In Jesus, they found someone willing to challenge the belief that only God could forgive, thereby making forgiveness also a human affair. Forgiveness interrupted the processes that seemed to govern human affairs and in this respect, was experienced as a miracle.[20] This remains our experience of forgiving as well: "forgiving attempts the seemingly impossible, to undo what has been done, and…it succeeds in making a new beginning where beginnings seemed to have been no longer possible."[21] It enables us to have a new relationship to time and thereby liberates us for hope. Without forgiving, acting for justice and love makes no sense, for we would have no hope. We would be ensnared in a web of relations and the consequences of actions wherein the disruption that comes from natality would be ineffective if not impossible.

BEYOND FORGIVENESS

But this is the point at which the difference between what Arendt understands as forgiveness and a more fundamental concept of mercy becomes relevant. Forgiving as she uses it represents an act in response to a given situation. In this understanding, forgiving is basically the same as pardoning or an act of judicial mercy. This is not an unusual take on these terms and is even seen in *Misericordiae Vultus*, where Pope Francis sometimes uses the terms *mercy, forgiveness*, and *pardon* interchangeably. But if forgiving is understood as this kind of action and located in a forensic context, we run up against limits, which Arendt describes in terms of the relationship between forgiveness and punishment.

Thinking forensically about forgiveness immediately locates the act of forgiving in the context of punishment. Judgment that a violation of the law has taken place entails punishment for that crime. In forgiving, that punishment is set aside; forgiving is, in this context, closely related with (the setting aside of) punishment. What this means in principle for Arendt is if an act is done that cannot be punished, neither can it be forgiven. Punishment and forgiveness "have in common that they attempt to put an end to something that without interference could go on endlessly." This means "that men are unable to forgive what they cannot punish and that they are unable to punish what has turned out to be unforgivable."[22] Some things we do are beyond forgiveness because they take us beyond punishment. But this is a moral sleight of hand.

Arendt is concerned here with something far more concrete than a forensic principle. She is responding to her historical situation as a German Jewish émigré working and living in the United States during and after the Third Reich. Her question was the challenge faced widely after 1945: How does one respond to the Holocaust? The punishment/forgiveness framework seemed to fail, a failure she testified to in her reporting on the trial, conviction, and execution of Adolf Eichmann.

Forgiveness was not possible because punishment failed, and punishment failed for two kinds of reasons: first, the acts involved were so far outside the realm of common human decency that they could not be understood and legally categorized adequately; and second, punishment and forgiveness are for a crime, but they apply to the perpetrator, that is, a person, and the Nazi culture made it possible for perpetrators to deny that they were responsible human agents. A person is punished, but the Nazi system worked according to mechanical principles wherein people were cogs in a machine of death and destruction.[23] Punishment failed, so forgiveness was out of the question—the category simply did not apply.

But does mercy fail as well? Our question here is not about forgiving the perpetrators but whether or not living mercifully makes sense in our situation of living after Auschwitz (Metz's preferred term to avoid any connotation of meaningfulness that attaches to the word holocaust as a burnt offering). As has been claimed earlier in this essay as well as in some of the essays in this volume, forgiveness is attached to particular acts, but mercy is a way of living in the world. One may speak of someone as having a forgiving personality, but even this designation is based on acts of the person observed by others. Mercy as a principle is revealed in actions, but its rational place is prior to those actions. Does living mercifully make sense after Auschwitz?

Metz does not address this question directly, but he may help us to find our own affirmative answer to it: yes, living mercifully does make sense, even after Auschwitz. Metz's thinking is deeply informed by his experience as a German Roman Catholic theologian who served in the Wehrmacht (he was pressed into service as a sixteen-year-old at the end of the war) and who feels particularly responsible for facing the world of and after Auschwitz. One way this is apparent is in the centrality of the problem of theodicy to his theology. For Metz, theodicy is not a matter of explaining why God allows evil to happen; neither is it about turning God's promise of justice and love into a guaranty of meaning that would allow us to turn our backs to Auschwitz as something beyond our understanding. He disdains any explanations that would let either himself or God avoid facing what happened by obscuring, explaining, or even trying to find the good in this evil. Auschwitz constitutes a dangerous memory, but at least in part, this is because Metz refuses to give up on God. For example, it still makes sense to pray to God: "We can pray *after* Auschwitz because there was prayer even *in*

Auschwitz."[24] He describes not so much a theodicy as a "mysticism of suffering unto God," putting us in the situation of Job who challenges God to be God. Theology after Auschwitz is not about explanations but about questions, the questions we put to ourselves and to God.

The connection to Job helps us translate these remarks into a response to the question of the meaningfulness of merciful living after Auschwitz. The Book of Job works in a forensic context, and Job's statement of his case in chapters 29–31, ending with a conditional oath of purity in his own defense, comes straight from the courtroom. But Job is not using the system of punishment/forgiveness that informs our legal proceedings. Law in Job—and in Judaism—is not a set of rules we posit in order to live securely and that stand outside us and teach and guide us as well as justify our punishment (the way laws are understood usually in our culture). Law is instead the Torah in which we have life and an expression of our relationship with God—the covenant. Job's challenging God to be God is asking him to return to the covenant God established with Israel. The word in Hebrew for this covenant faithfulness or steadfast love is *hesed*, a word that is also often translated as *mercy*.[25]

For Metz, covenant is crucial to understanding and carrying forward the Christian mission to what Arendt calls plural beings, that is, others in their otherness. As Metz writes in the essay in this volume, "1492—Through the Eyes of a European Theologian":

> From the very beginning, with its consciousness of mission, Christianity struggled for a culture of the recognition of the other. What was to be normative for this consciousness of mission was not Hellenistic thinking in terms of identity and assimilation, but the biblical notion of covenant, according to which, like is not known by like, rather, unlikes know one another by recognizing one another. (14)

As several of the writers in this volume emphasize, it is this recognition of otherness and the solidarity this recognition makes possible that characterize mercy and living mercifully.

Practically, the question of whether living mercifully makes sense after Auschwitz or at any time is a matter of how we live and act in the world. We saw previously that for Paul, a consequence of our eschatological hope is a rational principle of living *hos me*, "as not." We are called to live according to our hope in God's eschatological promise of justice and love even though the world is not full of mercy and our merciful actions do not always have the effects we intend. How can they, given the web of human relationships? But we act in hope, and it is mercy that liberates us for this hope.

This liberation to hope should not be understood as an escape from the past. It is not a matter of drawing a line under the past as over and done with and beyond the effects of our actions. To believe this would be to confine us to a notion of forgiveness as the mirror image of punishment, where punishment is understood as paying a debt and starting fresh. The past is not canceled out, and we are called to remember the victims of past injustice even when such memories are dangerous to the plausibility structures we erect to allow actions to flow smoothly. This is what Metz calls "remembrancing," the kind of memory work in which the past is allowed to interrupt the present rather than working through the past to reach "closure." Merciful living makes it possible and reasonable to carry the past with us in testimony to the radical temporal character of our hope that views history in terms of its disruptions.

NOTES

1. For more on this hope, see the essay by J. Matthew Ashley in this volume; also, Terry Eagleton, *Hope without Optimism* (New Haven, CT: Yale University Press, 2015).

2. Walter Benjamin, "On the Concept of History," in *Walter Benjamin: Selected Writings*, ed. Howard Eiland and Michael W. Jennings, vol. 4, *1938–1940*, trans. Edmund Jephcott et al. (Cambridge, MA: The Belknap Press of Harvard University Press, 2003), 397.

3. Johann Baptist Metz, "Hope as Imminent Expectation—or, The Struggle for Lost Time: Untimely Theses on Apocalyptic," in *Faith in History and Society: Toward a Practical Fundamental Theology*, ed. and trans. J. Matthew Ashley (New York: Crossroad Publishing, 2007), 158.

4. See, especially, 1 Cor 7; also, Giorgio Agamben, *The Time That Remains: A Commentary on the Letter to the Romans*, trans. Patricia Dailey (Stanford, CA: Stanford University Press, 2005); Letty M.

Russell, *Human Liberation in a Feminist Perspective: A Theology* (Philadelphia: The Westminster Press, 1974); and Steven T. Ostovich, "Pauline Eschatology: Thinking and Acting in the Time that Remains," in *Time: Limits and Constraints*, ed. Jo Alyson Parker, Paul A. Harris, and Christian Steineck, vol. 13, The Study of Time (Leiden/Boston: Brill, 2010), 307–27.

    5. See https://w2.vatican.va/content/francesco/en/apost_letters/documents/papa-francesco_bolla_20150411_misericordiae-vultus.html.

    6. See the essay by Johann Vento in this volume as well as what follows on the practice-character of mercy and the circular relationship between feeling and responding mercifully.

    7. Hannah Arendt, *The Human Condition*, 2nd ed. (Chicago: University of Chicago Press, 1958), 9–10.

    8. Ibid., 8; also 176.

    9. Ibid., 177; see also the essay by Michael Kirwan in this volume.

    10. Ibid., 247; see the essay by John Downey in this volume for a description by St. Francis of acting as giving birth.

    11. Hannah Arendt, *The Promise of Politics*, ed. Jerome Kohn (New York: Schocken Books, 2005), 108.

    12. Arendt, *The Human Condition*, 189, 222–23.

    13. Hannah Arendt, *Between Past and Future: Eight Exercises in Political Thought* (New York: Penguin Books, 1968), 151–52.

    14. Simone de Beauvoir similarly writes, "It is not true that the recognition of the freedom of others limits my own freedom: to be free is not to have the power to do anything you like; it is to be able to surpass the given toward an open future; the existence of others as a freedom defines my situation and is even the condition of my own freedom." *The Ethics of Ambiguity*, trans. Bernard Frechtman (New York: Citadel Press of Kensington Publishing Company, 1976), 91.

    15. Arendt, *The Human Condition*, 183.

    16. Ibid., 184.

    17. Ibid., 244.

    18. Ibid., 243–44.

    19. Ibid., 241.

    20. Ibid., 246.

    21. Arendt, *The Promise of Politics*, 58.

    22. Arendt, *The Human Condition*, 241.

23. Hannah Arendt, *Essays in Understanding 1930–1954: Formation, Exile, and Totalitarianism*, ed. Jerome Kohn (New York: Schocken Books, 1994), 232–47, 309–10; Hannah Arendt, *Responsibility and Judgment*, ed. Jerome Kohn (New York: Schocken Books, 2003), 23, 55, 95, 111. See also, Hannah Arendt, *Eichmann in Jerusalem: A Report on the Banality of Evil* (New York: Penguin Books, 2006).

24. Johann Baptist Metz, "Theology as Theodicy?" in *A Passion for God: The Mystical-Political Dimension of Christianity*, ed. and trans. J. Matthew Ashley (New York: Paulist Press, 1998), 63.

25. See, e.g., the refrain in Ps 136, where *hasdo* (or "his *hesed*-ness) is translated variously as "mercy" (NAB) and "steadfast love" (NRSV).

III

RECOGNITION

6

Bystander Mercy

Interrupting Sexual Violence in the "Culture of Indifference"

Johann M. Vento

> *No one has to do everything...everyone has to do something.*
>   —slogan of the Green Dot Bystander
>   Intervention Program[1]

INTRODUCTION

I am honored to have been trained in the Green Dot Bystander Intervention Program and part of its implementation on my university campus. Green Dot was founded by psychologist and violence prevention educator Dorothy J. Edwards at the University of Kentucky.[2] It seeks to create a change in the culture that brings about a reduction in the level of personal violence in our communities.[3] Edwards describes the motivation for her work with passion and urgency:

> I am not willing to let this world dull my senses to this issue.
> I am not willing to be swallowed by the apathy around me.
> I am not willing to pretend it is not horrifying that thousands

of women, children and men will be victims of sexual violence, partner violence, stalking and abuse every single day. I am defiant against a culture that tries to lull my soul into quiet complacency as our daughters and our sons—our wives and our sisters—face violence and the threat of violence every single day.[4]

So much of the time, this kind of passionate outrage and determination about these forms of injustice seem lost in a deafening silence of indifference. We trivialize sexual violence in various ways. We excuse boasting about it as "locker room talk." We take it for granted as part of an equally taken-for-granted structure of gendered power. We minimize its effects. We blame victims. We blame alcohol. We distance ourselves from the pain of victims. We stand by. We are indeed lulled into "quiet complacency," as Edwards says.

Sexual assault occurs in epidemic proportions in the United States. One in five women and one in seventy-one men have reported being raped. One in twenty men and women has experienced some form of sexual coercion other than rape in his or her lifetime. Of all female rape victims, 12.3 percent and 27.8 percent of male rape victims first experienced rape when they were under the age of ten. Rape is a factor in 68 percent of cases of domestic abuse in which a woman files for a protective order. In those same cases, 20 percent reported a pregnancy that had resulted from rape. Among college-aged women, 19 percent report experiencing some form of sexual assault while in college. Of all women victims of rape, 37.4 percent were first raped between the ages of eighteen and twenty-four.[5] Moreover, sexual assault in childhood, among other adverse childhood experiences, leaves victims at greater risk for a host of illnesses including heart disease, cancer, depression, and suicide attempts later in life.[6] These forms of violence are much more in the public consciousness in these past forty years—we know much more about them, and there are more resources devoted to serving those who have been affected by them. But the rates of such forms of violence have not gone down in that time.[7] Our awareness of the problem does nothing, in and of itself, to reduce the rates of these kinds of crimes. This is a key insight of the bystander intervention movement in violence prevention, and has led to a move from teaching about the prevalence of sexual violence to training bystanders to intervene. The preventive action of bystanders is key to reduction in rates of sexual violence. The indifference and/or inaction of bystanders is a major factor in the ongoing prevalence of sexual violence.[8]

What might insights from bystander intervention programs like Green Dot contribute to our theological reflection on this issue?[9] What are the contours of mercy in the face of epidemic levels of sexual violence? Keeping in mind Pope Francis's call for mercy in the face of a "culture of indifference," I want to explore both our complacency and indifference as well as how we might create in its place what Francis names a "culture of encounter" regarding sexual violence.[10] Jon Sobrino, in his 1991 work, *The Principle of Mercy: Taking the Crucified People from the Cross*, argues that we cannot limit ourselves to the level of speaking of "works of mercy," but rather that Christian theology needs to take account of the very "structure" of mercy itself, which he says "consists in making someone else's pain our very own and allowing that pain to move us to respond."[11] But how do we do this? A pervasive moral callousness in our culture inures us to sexual violence. How do we wear down this moral callus and face the suffering engendered by sexual violence? How do we feel the pain of another in this context and allow this pain to move us to a merciful response?

When I encountered the Green Dot strategy, I became interested in practice theory and what it might contribute to theological reflection about this very problem—about our "stuckness" in moral callousness about sexual violence. I am primarily interested in the formative nature of practice, both of practices that form us into moral callousness and those that have the potential to form in us resistance to violence. An understanding of practice as formative operates as an unexplored practice theory in the political theologies of both Dorothee Soelle and Johann Baptist Metz. In Flora Keshgegian's book *A Time for Hope*, in which she outlines practices that can nurture hope in Christians of this age, Keshgegian relates something that she once heard Dorothee Soelle say in a public lecture and that never left her. Keshgegian recounts,

> [Soelle] likened the character of hope to a baby beginning to walk. It is in and through getting up on her feet and taking the steps that a baby learns to walk. Similarly with hope, we will learn to hope anew as we practice hope. The practice of hope is a process. It requires risk as well as boldness. Indeed, there is a miraculous quality to it, not unlike the

miracle of a baby learning to walk or talk or laugh. The miracle of hope is experienced in the practice of it, not in absolute guarantees.[12]

Dorothee Soelle addresses the formative role of practice many times in her work, noting that knowing about the problems, knowing about the suffering of the other, is not enough to produce a practice of solidarity, given how formed we are socially to avoid suffering and medicate ourselves against it. She argues that faith and hope for a different reality can only come about through resistance itself. That is, practices of resistance themselves can form in us the capacity to have hope and to continue to resist.[13] Metz argues for the function of the narrated Christian *memoria* in the formation of solidarity—that *memoria* that will allow us to engage with the countless other memories of suffering with open eyes, allowing that suffering to have authority for our life of discipleship. Metz also writes, "One is not introduced to the world of religion by religious studies nor to the world of morality by ethics. Before one can develop a self-conscious relationship to them, one has to practice, one has to become biographically engaged."[14]

In his call for a return to mercy, Pope Francis also emphasizes the centrality of practice. In *Misericordiae Vultus*, which proclaims the Jubilee Year of Mercy, Francis makes clear his understanding of the formative function of practice to break through indifference toward the suffering. He talks about the activities of the Year of Mercy: the works of mercy, striving for justice, and all actions that "restore dignity to all from whom it has been robbed" as that which will "reawaken our conscience" and form in us more and more the ability to feel and respond (*Misericordiae Vultis* 15–16).[15] It is not that our consciences are reawakened and then we respond. For Francis, it is a circular relationship, and the practice itself forms in us the capacity for feeling and then ever greater practical response.

In this essay, I begin with a discussion of moral callousness regarding sexual violence. To explore how we might "reawaken our conscience" about sexual violence, I will present in brief the contours of French sociologist Pierre Bourdieu's practice theory, especially his understanding of habitus, as a helpful diagnostic tool to articulate the power and depth, the durability, of moral callousness. Further, I will offer insights from Bourdieu's feminist interpreters, who will point us toward a way of taking this durability seriously, while also giving us hope that we can resist it. I argue that the practice of mercy vis à vis sexual violence involves engaging in formative practices of resistance that have the capacity to shape a "culture of encounter" out of the "culture of indifference." Specifically, I will highlight key features of the Green Dot Bystander Intervention Program that offer insight into how we can face the problem of sexual violence in its full negativity and actively work to keep everyone in our communities safe from it.

MORAL CALLOUSNESS AND SEXUAL VIOLENCE

Mary Pellauer, in her work on violence against women, uses the term *moral callousness* to refer to the failure to feel for the suffering of the other. She demonstrates the aptness of the image of a callus as she fleshes out this evocative metaphor:

> A callus is precisely an area which is tough, horny, hardened, *unfeeling*; the synonyms slide readily from the physical sense of hardened into the larger human ones of unresponsiveness: thick-skinned, impervious, inured, insensible; blind to, deaf to, dead to; neglectful, inattentive, unsusceptible. This range of meanings has to do with our feelings, our capacity to be touched by, to be sensitive to the human reality in question. In a callus the healthy transmission of messages along nerve fibers does not function; calluses neither receive nor send messages to and from the central nervous system.[16]

In a recent case of campus rape at Stanford University, one that became famous because of widespread sharing about it on social media, we see one particularly glaring, shocking instance of such moral callousness toward a victim of rape. In his letter to the court appealing for a light sentence for his son, the father of the convicted rapist argued that his son should not have to suffer what he considered disproportionate punishment and long-term negative consequences for what he called, "twenty minutes of action."[17] His son had been caught in the act of raping an unconscious woman in an alley behind a dumpster. He called it "twenty minutes of action." This turned out to be a successful attempt by a father to get his son out of the consequences of his actions, as, in fact, his son did receive what many perceived to be a shockingly minimal sentence for this crime. Such a characterization of a brutal violent crime would not have the currency it does if it were not for a cultural context in which sexual violence is routinely minimized, trivialized, and/or blamed on the victim.

Not all failures of solidarity with victims are quite as obvious and publicly self-protective as this one. Most often the moral callousness on the part of ordinary people toward victims of sexual violence is more subtle and muted, but nonetheless pervasive and powerful. A stifling sense of the inevitability of sexual violence endures. We find ourselves unable to face suffering, to allow ourselves the pain of it, and to live in solidarity with those who suffer it, including when we ourselves are counted in that number. Therefore, trivialization, denial, and blaming the victim govern our response. Patriarchal patterns of gender relations in society form in us the sense that the violation of women and children is to be expected and, on a certain level, justified.[18] Unlike any other form of violent crime, there is an almost knee-jerk reaction to blame the victim, as in "What was she wearing?" "Had she been drinking?" or "What was she doing out at that hour?" When men are the victims of sexual assault, patriarchally constructed understandings of masculinity render such crimes practically invisible.[19] These attitudes, tightly interwoven in the fabric of our society, continue to thrive unchallenged, because they so often escape explicit acknowledgment and expression. Margaret Miles describes this situation, regarding violence against women in particular, comparing the relatively obvious exploitative elements of our society with the more insidious ones:

> The most pervasive foundations of violence against women are so ordinary, so unexceptional, and therefore so unnoticed that they are seldom challenged. Pornography...may be enormously important as the major eroticization of violence in our culture, but there are other rationalizations of and support for violence against women. These are more superficial in that they lie more on the surface of American culture; at the same time they are more foundational in that they are built into the assumptions and institutional structures of American culture

in the family and child-rearing, in educational institutions, and in churches, synagogues, and government.[20]

Societal assumptions about sexual violence attempt to contain and isolate these crimes by characterizing them as the aberrant acts of a very few individuals. Studies show however, that the attitudes and motivations of perpetrators are not unrelated to general attitudes about women, children, and inviolability, but rather are logical extensions of them. One such study, which analyzed the attitudes toward rape among university students, notes that these attitudes were similar to the attitudes of convicted rapists. The study concludes that their findings support "the contention that rape is an extension of normal attitudes and socialization practices in our society rather than totally the product of a sick and aberrant mind."[21] For many people who truly do lament sexual violence, there is a sense of helplessness and powerlessness to do anything about it. The problem seems so big, and words and actions seem to get lost in this overarching culture of indifference.

UNDERSTANDING MORAL CALLOUSNESS: INSIGHTS FROM BOURDIEU'S NOTION OF *HABITUS*

French sociologist Pierre Bourdieu argues that we are formed into a habitus, a set of dispositions representing deeply ingrained patterns of perception and behavior, taste, verbal manner, and physical comportment. The habitus is self-generating—and constantly regenerating itself. It is always evolving in response to external stimuli and is "capable of producing a multitude of different practices."[22] He speaks of the habitus as "an acquired system of generative schemes objectively adjusted to the particular conditions in which it is constituted" and that "engenders all the thoughts, all the perceptions, and all the actions consistent with those conditions, and no others."[23] Indeed, Bourdieu has an all-encompassing sense of the reach and effects of habitus. Moreover, for him, the process of the formation of habitus is entirely unconscious. For others who are more closely aligned with the Aristotelian understanding of the term, *habitus* refers to a specific set of dispositions and skills that can be purposefully formed through conscious, concerted

113

effort of one's own. For Bourdieu, this is not the case. For him, one's habitus is formed at a preconscious, prereflective level, although it is continually regenerated by one's own actions, which are first and foremost conditioned by the habitus. On this point, Bourdieu has been amply criticized for seeming to negate or at least downplay the role of conscious human agency. In response to such criticisms, he argues that habitus does not determine action, but instead is a "durably installed generative principle of regulated improvisation."[24] It is not that there is no human agency, but rather that agency is always enacted through the habitus, which is formed socially and preconsciously.

Habitus encompasses the sense of one's place in the social settings one inhabits. The larger setting is referred to as a "field," and each field has its own unspoken set of norms that interact with and form the habitus of individuals within that field. Within any given field, say of the theological academy, the aristocracy, the working class, the military, the sports team, the church, there operates a unique store of cultural capital that actors within that field compete to possess. Bourdieu uses the metaphor of a game, with its distinct set of rules, to describe a field. The rules do not determine the actions of the players, but provide the constraints under which actors act. Actors within a specific field internalize the norms, both spoken and unspoken. According to Peter Jackson, "For Bourdieu it is the informal and unspoken structures that constitute the most effective constraints on action because they operate at the level of the unconscious or semi-conscious. They constitute what he defines as the prevailing '*doxa*': 'the silent experience of the world.'"[25] For Bourdieu, the *doxa*, or as Terry Eagleton characterizes it, "that which goes without saying" in any given social field, serves powerfully to inculcate and quietly enforce social inequalities.[26]

Habitus operates on the level of collectivity to produce (and reproduce) social conditions, which, in turn, produce habitus in individuals, whose practices, in turn, form (and re-form) social conditions: "In short, the habitus, the product of history, produces individual and collective practices, and hence history, in accordance with the schemes engendered by history."[27] Peter Jackson puts it this way: "The habitus plays a central role in the durability of hierarchies. It is the means through which the arbitrary is comprehended as 'natural' and even 'inevitable.' It determines what is imaginable and unimaginable and thus what is possible and what is impossible in the everyday flow of social life."[28]

In cases of social inequality, Bourdieu speaks of a symbolic domination (as opposed to domination through actual physical force) that produces a particular habitus in individuals (either of dominance or of subservience) and is constantly reproduced by the practices enacted by those individuals. According to this understanding, although domination can be enacted through explicit use of force, it achieves its stability, its perdurance, much more through "symbolic" force, that is, through the assumptions, choices, actions, tastes, and so forth, of the dominant and the dominated. Speaking of gender relations and the symbolic domination that keeps in place both male dominance and female subjection, he argues,

> The effect of symbolic domination (whether ethnic, gender, cultural, or linguistic, etcetera) is exerted not in the pure logic of knowing consciousness but through the schemes of perception, appreciation, and action that are constitutive of *habitus* and which, below the level of the decisions of consciousness and the controls of the will, set up a cognitive relationship that is profoundly obscure to itself.[29]

I appreciate Bourdieu's strong theory of the social structuring of practice and the capacity of his work to theorize the entrenched, and in many frustrating ways, unchanging patterns of social domination. Regarding the problem of sexual violence and moral callousness toward it, our patterns of minimization, trivialization, blaming the victim, and so on, seem stubbornly resistant to change. We continually downplay the reality of sexual violence and its full negativity. A realistic sense of the suffering that results from this violence and the ability truly to lament it seem continually to slip from our grasp. Solidarity with and mercy toward victims is elusive as our patterned forms of moral callousness structure our thoughts and actions. We are stuck in the culture of indifference.

Feminist sociologists who engage Bourdieu's work, while they critique certain aspects of it from a feminist perspective, also appreciate the capacity of his understanding of habitus to describe the "stuckness" of social domination, its remarkable ability to perdure, despite the passage of time and apparent social changes. As Bourdieu himself says, others theorize how things change; he wants to theorize how they stay the same. Steph Lawler puts it this way:

In the face of a contemporary political and theoretical emphasis on an easy plasticity and change, I think Bourdieu's work is important in reminding us that pessimism is not the same as determination; that resistance takes many forms; that in any case, for many groups of people, change is very difficult to effect, no matter how much they resist.[30]

FORMING A HABITUS OF MERCY

While I do not want to lose the power of Bourdieu's theory so aptly to theorize this "stuckness," I want also to speak of the possibility of the conscious formation of habitus. In fact, the intellectual trajectory that influences the development of Bourdieu's thought on habitus, from Aristotle through Merleau-Ponty and Marcel Mauss, itself *does* theorize habitus as consciously formable. The work of anthropologist Talal Asad on habitus, solidly within this trajectory of thought, points to how persons may intentionally cultivate certain dispositions through a program of discipline of the body and emotions. He alludes to athletic and musical training as examples of a kind of second nature that may be formed through use of repetitive training. For Asad, what we choose to do with our bodies is formative of habitus.[31]

Further, while they appreciate the capacity of Bourdieu's theory to account for the durability of social relations due to the largely unconscious process of the structuring and continual restructuring of habitus, contemporary feminist commentators on Bourdieu believe that he "overplays the unconscious impulses and aspects of habitus"[32] and call for an understanding of habitus that can "recuperate the reflective and creative aspects of practice."[33] Some see a possibility for this within Bourdieu's theory. For him, there is normally a compatibility between habitus and field, that is, between the "feel for the game" and the game itself. But, according to Lisa Adkins, for Bourdieu, this compatibility is not inevitable; it can break down. The field sets certain limits on practice, but agents' actions shape the field, so habitus and field feed into one another. Most often this creates durability. Adkins, among other feminist sociologists, appreciates this, but wants also to speak of the possibility of change, and specifically, the possibility of consciously chosen practices that can form a different kind of habitus, one of resistance to social domination, for instance. She notes that in his later work, Bourdieu does admit of the possibility of self-reflexivity and social change that can be brought on by a "lack of fit" between the habitus and the field (context) in which one finds oneself operating.[34] Therefore, while Bourdieu is primarily concerned with describing how things stay the same, his later work leaves more of an opening to theorizing self-reflexive, conscious, deliberate acts of forming a different kind of habitus.

Others feel it is necessary to go beyond Bourdieu to find this possibility. Theologian Mark Lewis Taylor posits the potential of a habitus of resistance to domination, raising the possibility that Bourdieu's basic theory of practice can be elaborated in such a way as to account for formation for resistance to injustice. Taylor argues that

> there are numerous studies of oppressed groups' awareness of their suffering, and of what might be called a *habitus* of resistance, a somatized relationality of struggle to adapt Bourdieu's notions, all in contrast to a mere *habitus* of acquiescence. This somatized relationality of struggle is at odds with, even if never completely free from, a [habitus of acquiescence to] domination.[35]

While Bourdieu's understanding of habitus helps us to understand the true negativity and deep stability, the depth and the breadth of our socialization into moral callousness toward sexual violence, Taylor's caveat is also needed: the possibility of a degree of freedom from this socialization—the possibility of forming a habitus of resistance. In the face of the epidemic of sexual violence and the pervasiveness and power of moral callousness toward it, and recalling Sobrino's understanding of mercy as feeling the pain of another as our very own and out of that experience, responding, can we speak of forming a habitus of mercy toward sexual violence?

INTERRUPTING SEXUAL VIOLENCE

Informed by Bourdieu about the nature of our "stuckness" in moral callousness about sexual violence, and encouraged by his interpreters who also see the possibility of forming a new kind of habitus, I want to outline what I believe would be the contours of a practice of resistance to sexual violence. I will use as an example the bystander violence intervention program called Green Dot. The practices involved in the formation of a community of support and resistance are the very practices that wake us up collectively and heal all of us from the "monotonous victoriousness of reality as it has come to be," to use one of my favorite expressions of Metz.[36]

The Green Dot philosophy echoes much of what I recalled from Metz and Soelle at the beginning of this essay, that merely knowing about injustice does not necessarily equip us to resist it. In creating Green Dot, Edwards built on the realization that merely teaching others the staggering statistics about the prevalence of violence does not bring about a decline in its numbers. It does not create cultural change. She set about to create a strategy that would teach people their own power literally to interrupt power-based personal violence incident by incident, betting that when enough people begin to do this in an intentional and consistent way, there will eventually be a "tipping point" where the numbers of actual acts of violence will decrease and the thoughts and acts of the culture vis-à-vis power-based personal violence will change. Edwards seeks to change the culture—a culture of apathy about epidemic levels of these types of violence—to a culture of empathy and action.[37]

The Green Dot strategy is a formation process. It invites reflection on power-based personal violence in a personal way. Using a series of reflective and imaginative exercises, it nurtures a sense of empathy and urgency in is participants as the foundation for training in a set of practices to interrupt violence. Participants are trained to "do Green Dots," that is, to intervene in some way whenever they see or suspect that an instance of violence is about to happen. Participants are led through a training process to identify actions they could safely and effectively take if they see a woman clearly too drunk to consent to being led upstairs at a party, if they see a husband behaving aggressively toward his wife at a shopping mall, or if they see a mom about to beat a child, to name a few examples. Part of the genius of this program is that it does not try to encourage people to aspire to some unrealistic ideal of heroism. Rather, it encourages participants to be honest about their own personalities, proclivities, and potential barriers to action and to identify for themselves actions they could realistically see themselves doing. The training allows them to practice these strategies in groups. Further, once the training is over, participants form a community of people who swap stories about the Green Dots they have done. The Green Dot community provides a continual process of formation, encouraging participants to stay with and enact their commitment to ending violence "one green dot at a time." Green Dot has been widely implemented on college campuses, in high schools, and in middle schools, among the armed forces and in many other contexts. There are indications that the Green Dot strategy is effective in reducing incidents of violence. A study by the Centers for Disease Control and Prevention has found that high schools that implement the Green Dot strategy have seen a 50 percent reduction in incidents of power-based personal violence.[38]

What can theological reflection about the epidemic of sexual violence learn from the practical example of Green Dot? First, it is rooted in outrage. The quote from Dorothy Edwards with which I began this essay makes clear the passionate indignation about personal violence that is the impetus for the creation of Green Dot. The Green Dot strategy consciously seeks to create an opening for this kind of passion in its participants. Next, it involves formative practice. It nurtures this passion and gives it hope, by giving participants practical, doable strategies to interrupt violence. Finally, it creates and sustains a community of resistance that provides ongoing formation and encouragement and creates hope and energy for continuing to interrupt patterns of violence. In a Bourdieuan understanding, the repetition of this pattern of behavior (doing Green Dots) has the potential to interact with this new field (the Green Dot community) to form a new habitus, one that can reproduce itself socially and create a new durability. This is a sociological way of describing the kind of cultural change that Dorothy Edwards has envisioned with this strategy.

In theological terms, it suggests to us that in the face of moral callousness about sexual violence, we must be formed to mercy. We must teach ourselves, through practice, to open ourselves to suffering, to consciously nurture a sense of its lamentability, and to act to practical effect. Recalling what Pope Francis has noted about the capacity of practices in the interest of the dignity of each person to "reawaken our conscience" regarding the suffering of the other, mercy itself emerges as an ongoing formative process of freeing ourselves from indifference and tutoring ourselves and one another in our community, in practical action, to interrupt the dynamics of sexual violence.

CONCLUSION

I want to conclude by introducing a few nuances. I wish to avoid an overly rationalistic or mechanistic understanding that would characterize the process of formation as a recipe that, when appropriate ingredients are used and directions correctly followed, will yield a predictable response. I am speaking of something that, while essentially social, is also deeply personal, and in the thought of political theology, profoundly mystical. I do not mean for this to sound mechanistic or utopian, but rather urgent, insistent, and hopeful about the possibility of intentional formation of a habitus of mercy.

In this regard, it is important to keep in *tension* Bourdieu's theorizing about the durability of habitus, on the one hand, and the conscious formation or restructuring of habitus, on the other. These remain in tension not just theoretically but in individuals (always rooted in the social), in our concrete embodied experience. Whatever measure of consciously formed disposition is possible will exist alongside of and in dynamic relationship with those subterranean aspects of habitus that remain obscure to us. In terms specific to the question of sexual violence, this will mean *both* a conscious attempt to cultivate a practice of mercy with victims *and* a humbling and salutary reminder of (in Bourdieuan terms) "the social world," in this case, the "culture of indifference" toward sexual violence. We will continue to some degree (perhaps to a very great degree) to embody dispositions to sexual violence and to moral callousness toward it, even as we consciously strive to resist them.

In an attempt to account for the durability of moral callousness about sexual violence, I have attempted to argue for the possibility of another kind of formation, a *re-formation*, that can resist this callousness and replace it with resistance. Since the patterns of domination are stable only because symbolic domination is constantly regenerating itself, there is hope that there can be a break in that regeneration. It follows that the social patterns of moral callousness formed and fed by the practices that keep it in place can be interrupted. But that break will result only from a deliberate, vigilant, stable set of practices in community that form and reinforce the dispositions that can resist and break the pattern. The formation of dispositions of mercy should work in the same way as the processes that form and re-form moral callousness.

The Green Dot strategy contributes to our understanding of the contours of mercy regarding the epidemic of sexual violence. It shows us what formation for a "culture of encounter" to counter the "culture of indifference" might look like. In concrete terms, a set of practices that engender passionate outrage about violence and empathy toward victims; that nurture hope that change is possible; that teach practical, realistic strategies to equip participants to interrupt violence when they see it; and that create communities of ongoing formation to keep up the work of resistance has the potential to form us to mercy, that is, to recall Sobrino once more, to form in us the capacity of making "someone else's pain our very own and allowing that pain to move us to respond."[39]

NOTES

1. See *Ending Violence One Green Dot at a Time, Instructor Manual*, © 2009 Dorothy J. Edwards, PhD. Used with permission, and available at https://alteristic.org/services/green-dot/.

2. Green Dot is now independent of the University of Kentucky under the name Alteristic. See https://alteristic.org/services/green-dot/.

3. Green Dot uses the phrase *power-based personal violence* as an inclusive term for all forms of personal violence it seeks to eradicate: sexual violence, partner violence, bullying, stalking, and the like. In this essay, I will use *power-based personal violence* when referring to this larger field of forms of violence, and sexual violence when speaking specifically about that phenomenon.

4. Edwards, *Ending Violence*, 1.

5. "Sexual Violence: Data Sources—Quick Facts," Centers for Disease Control and Prevention, accessed on September 25, 2016, http://www.cdc.gov/violenceprevention/sexualviolence/datasources.html.

6. "About the CDC-Kaiser ACE Study," Centers for Disease Control and Prevention, accessed on September 25, 2016, https://www.cdc.gov/violenceprevention/acestudy/about.html.

7. Barbara Nagel, Hisako Matsuo, Kevin P. McIntyre, and Nancy Morrison, "Attitudes toward Victims of Rape: Effect of Gender, Race, Religion, and Social Class," *Journal of Interpersonal Violence* 20, no. 6 (June 2005): 725.

8. Ann L. Coker, Heather L. Bush et al., "Multi-College Bystander Intervention Evaluation for Violence Prevention," *American Journal of Preventive Medicine* 50, no. 3 (March 2016): 295–302.

9. Green Dot seeks to train people to be active bystanders, that is, to intervene actively to prevent individual instances of power-based personal violence. For an extended theological treatment of passive bystanding to injustice and its relation to apathy and privilege, see Elizabeth T. Vasko, *Beyond Apathy: A Theology for Bystanders* (Minneapolis: Fortress Press, 2015).

10. For Pope Francis on the culture of indifference and the culture of encounter, see among others, Pope Francis, "For a Culture of Encounter," September 13, 2016, https://w2.vatican.va/content/francesco/en/cotidie/2016/documents/papa-francesco-cotidie_20160913_for-a-culture-of-encounter.html.

11. Jon Sobrino, *The Principle of Mercy: Taking the Crucified People from the Cross* (Maryknoll, NY: Orbis, 1994), 10.

12. Flora Keshgegian, *A Time for Hope: Practices for Living in Today's World* (New York: Continuum, 2006), 188.

13. Dorothee Soelle, *The Silent Cry: Mysticism and Resistance*, trans. Barbara and Martin Rumscheidt (Minneapolis: Fortress Press, 2001), 204.

14. Johann Baptist Metz, "In the Pluralism of Religious and Cultural Worlds: Notes toward a Theological and Political Paradigm," *Cross Currents* 49, no. 2 (Summer 1999): 234.

15. See https://w2.vatican.va/content/francesco/en/apost_letters/documents/papa-francesco_bolla_20150411_misericordiae-vultus.html.

16. Mary Pellauer, "Moral Callousness and Moral Sensitivity: Violence against Women," in *Women's Consciousness, Women's Conscience*, ed. Barbara Hilkert Andolsen, Christine E. Gudorf, and Mary D. Pellauer (San Francisco: Harper and Row, 1987), 48–49.

17. Liam Stack, "Light Sentence for Brock Turner in Stanford Rape Case Draws Outrage," *The New York Times*, June 6, 2016, accessed November 13, 2016, http://www.nytimes.com/2016/06/07/

us/outrage-in-stanford-rape-case-over-dueling-statements-of-victim-and
-attackers-father.html.

18. Jane P. Sheldon and Sandra L. Parent, "Clergy's Attitudes and Attributions of Blame toward Female Rape Victims," *Violence against Women* 8, no. 2 (February 2002): 239. See also Rocco L. Caprano, "Disconnected Lives: Men, Masculinity, and Rape Prevention," *New Directions for Student Services* 65 (Spring 1994): 21–33; Sandra L. Caron and D. Bruce Carter, "The Relationship among Sex Role Orientation, Egalitarianism, Attitudes toward Sexuality, and Attitudes toward Violence against Women," *Journal of Social Psychology* 137, no. 5 (1997): 568–87; and N. Tatiana Masters, "'My Strength is Not for Hurting': Men's Anti-Rape Websites and their Construction of Masculinity and Male Sexuality," *Sexualities* 13, no. 1 (2010): 33–46.

19. Rhys Price-Robertson, "Child Sexual Abuse, Masculinity, and Fatherhood," *Journal of Family Studies* 18, no. 203 (December 2012): 138. See also M. Kia-Keating, L. Sorsoli, and F. K. Grossman, "Relational Challenges and Recovery Processes in Male Survivors of Childhood Sexual Assault," *Journal of Interpersonal Violence* 25, no. 4 (April 2010): 666–83; Sasha Gear, "Behind the Bars of Masculinity: Male Rape and Homophobia in and about South African Men's Prisons," *Sexualities* 10, no. 2 (2007): 209–27; and Leslee R. Kassing and Loreto R. Prieto, "The Rape Myth and Blame-Based Beliefs of Counselors in Training toward Male Victims of Rape," *Journal of Counseling and Development* 81 (Fall 2003): 455–61.

20. Margaret R. Miles, "Violence against Women in the Historical Christian West and North American Secular Culture: The Visual and Textual Evidence," in *Shaping New Vision: Gender and Values in American Culture*, ed. Clarissa W. Atkinson, Constance H. Buchanan, and Margaret R. Miles (Ann Arbor: UMI Research Press, 1987), 15.

21. Neil Malamuth and Seymour Feshbach, "Testing Hypotheses regarding Rape: Exposure to Sexual Violence, Sex Differences, and the 'Normality' of Rapists," *Journal of Research on Personality* 14 (1980): 134.

22. Peter Jackson, "Pierre Bourdieu, the 'Cultural Turn' and International History," *Review of International Studies* 34 (2008): 165.

23. Pierre Bourdieu, *Outline of a Theory of Practice* (Cambridge: Cambridge University Press, 1977), 95.

24. Ibid., 78.

25. Jackson, "Pierre Bourdieu," 167.

26. Ibid.

27. Bourdieu, *Outline of a Theory of Practice*, 82.

28. Jackson, "Pierre Bourdieu," 165.

29. Pierre Bourdieu, *Masculine Domination*, trans. Richard Nice (Stanford, CA: Stanford University Press, 2001), 37.

30. Steph Lawler, "Rules of Engagement: Habitus, Power, and Resistance," in *Feminism after Bourdieu*, ed. Lisa Adkins and Beverley Skeggs (Malden, MA: Blackwell, 2004), 124–25.

31. Talal Asad, *Formations of the Secular: Christianity, Islam, and Modernity* (Stanford, CA: Stanford University Press, 2003), 89.

32. Diane Reay, "'It's all Becoming a Habitus': Beyond the Habitual Use of Habitus in Educational Research," *British Journal of Sociology of Education* 25, no. 4 (2004): 437.

33. Ibid. Reay is here quoting Nick Crossley, "Fish, Field, Habitus and Madness: The First Wave Mental Health Users Movement in Great Britain," *British Journal of Sociology* 50, no. 4 (1999): 647–70.

34. Lisa Adkins, "Reflexivity: Freedom or Habit of Gender," in *Feminism after Bourdieu*, ed. Lisa Adkins and Beverley Skeggs (Malden, MA: Blackwell, 2004), 197.

35. Mark Lewis Taylor, *The Theological and the Political: On the Weight of the World* (Minneapolis: Fortress Press, 2011), 119.

36. Johann Baptist Metz, *The Emergent Church: The Future of Christianity in a Post-Bourgeois World* (New York: Crossroad Publishing, 1986), 99.

37. Edwards, *Ending Violence*, 4.

38. *Green Dot, etcetera*, accessed November 13, 2016, https://www.livethegreendot.com.

39. Sobrino, *The Principle of Mercy*, 10.

7

Facing Religious Neighbors

Nostra Aetate Fifty Years On

John N. Sheveland

The Samaritan descends into the dust and dirt of the street, touches and binds up the wounds of the one fallen among robbers, and also pays for his care. [Pope] Francis speaks of a mysticism of coexistence and encounter, of embracing and supporting one another, of participating in a caravan of solidarity, in a sacred pilgrimage; he speaks of a mystical and contemplative fraternity, which "knows how to see the sacred grandeur of our neighbor, of finding God in every human being" (*EG* 92). Or—Johann Baptist Metz put it— this is not a mysticism of closed eyes, but rather a mysticism of open eyes, which becomes a mysticism of helping hands.[1]

These words by Walter Kasper reflect Pope Francis's pivot toward mercy and tenderness that, during his young papacy, raises to consciousness in a historically unprecedented manner the activity and lifestyle of dialogue, a theme prevalent throughout the new Pope's writings, speeches, and homilies (see *Evangelii Gaudium* 88).[2] While we can look to 1965 and the Second Vatican Council's Declaration on the Church's Relationship to Non-Christian Religions (*Nostra Aetate*) as a watershed document that empowered Christians to perceive similarities in followers of other religious paths and to engage them in dialogue, it is also true that the church's reception over fifty years of this invitation to dialogue reveals a development and growth in understanding, not its completion. We can be prepared to acknowledge the undisputed value and historical contribution that *Nostra Aetate* was and remains.

Even so, we are also prepared to inquire, fifty years on, after a fuller scope and force of the document here and now. That is, from a Christian theological perspective, what is the force of dialogue as an activity and orientation in a world of living beings, as an activity that transpires not between religions that lack subjectivity, but between human persons? More pointedly, to whom are we responsible, in dialogue, and what are the human ends to which dialogue shall be purposed? How prominent within dialogue do we wish to make mercy and other forms of redemptive activity, both as a goal for dialogue as well as, more simply, the material expression of what the declaration's first paragraph refers to as the goal of "fellowship" and the promotion of unity and love among all nations (*Nostra Aetate* 1)?[3] This essay seeks to address that underdeveloped possibility.

Johann Baptist Metz hinted at the value of this line of work, even if he was not himself engaging comparative religious scholarship or developing theologies of religious pluralism. He wrote of an "indirect ecumenism of religions," by which he announced the possibility of religious believers from across a variety of traditions coming together to engage in dialogue. Such a dialogue would not be over abstract ideas or elegant intellectual debates, but around how best to engage each other's wisdom in order to develop, collaboratively, new and transformative forms of praxis in the face of unjust suffering in the world due to racism, xenophobia, ethnoreligious nationalism, and the like.[4] Sadly, fifty years after its promulgation, we have yet to see a robust reflection on *Nostra Aetate* centered around political theology's concern for suffering or an interreligious praxis developed in response.

In one of the more well-known contributions of the Council, the declaration's second paragraph stipulates the church's positive recognition of the truths evident of other religious ways:

> The Catholic Church rejects nothing that is true and holy in these religions. She regards with sincere reverence those

ways of conduct and of life, those precepts and teachings which, though differing in many aspects from the ones she holds and sets forth, nonetheless often reflect a ray of that Truth which enlightens all men [sic.]. Indeed, she proclaims, and ever must proclaim Christ "the way, the truth, and the life" (John 14:6), in whom men may find the fullness of religious life, in whom God has reconciled all things to Himself.

The Church, therefore, exhorts her sons, that through dialogue and collaboration with the followers of other religions, carried out with prudence and love and in witness to the Christian faith and life, they recognize, preserve and promote the good things, spiritual and moral, as well as the socio-cultural values found among these men. (*Nostra Aetate* 2)

What could it mean, fifty years on, to posit that the teachings of other religious traditions might reflect a "ray" of the "Truth" that enlightens all people? Is the category "ray" formal and deliberately vague, or might it have material content from which Christians can learn, compare with their own understandings, and even enact? In the Latin text, the truth in which "other religions" participate as potential "rays," is *Veritas* with a capital V, namely, the declaration that *Christ* is the way, the truth, and the life, the one in whom all human persons find their fulfillment. While the declaration clearly intends to express deep respect for a plurality of forms of revelation affirmed to be present in other religions and that these forms are differentiated, the foundation of that respect is the implication that the truth of these forms of revelation are *participative*, derived from the plenary and unique truth of Christ (*Veritas*) revealed in the person and work of Jesus Christ.

What follows in this essay probes three arguments. First, the declaration's vocation to human unity expressed in *Nostra Aetate* 1 and throughout other conciliar documents—notably in *Gaudium et Spes* 1—provides a norm to determine precisely in what the category "rays of divine truth" consists, namely, those teachings that enable persons to perceive and act upon the human unity and solidarity of which they are endowed by their Creator. Admittedly, interpretation of *Nostra Aetate* in the literature has not given full attention to this connection between sections 1 and 2 and, more specifically, to the possibility that section 2's claim about "rays" of divine truth might be normed by section 1's affirmation of the solidarity of all in the presence of the divine. This connection renders more explicit the role of Christ as redeemer and infers that participative rays of divine truth discovered in other religious traditions are likewise "truth" insofar as they are experienced to be redemptive. The particularity of Christ as the locus of truth expressed in section 2 necessitates in Christian community explicit performances of solidarity and reconciliation: Christ achieved our peace and yet was a victim thereby, and the revelation of God in Christ not only discloses the reconciliation accomplished but also the depth of human dysfunction and division from which persons in Christ are redeemed. This proposal seeks to pivot away from a wooden reading of *Nostra Aetate* 2 as simply conveying theological inclusivism, and it seeks to pivot toward a reception of section 2 as animated by the particularity of Christ inclusive of a felt sense of vocation to human unity that, in our time, may be rediscovered and expressed in partnerships with religious neighbors.

To pilot this proposal, the essay enacts partnerships with the voices of contemporary Buddhist scholar John Makransky and contemporary Orthodox Rabbi Irving "Yitz" Greenberg, both of whom may provide content to the promising category "rays of divine truth." In this way, the declaration may be seen to invite us to sincerely revere other religions not in an abstract theology of religions—which may serve important doctrinal needs but accomplishes little by way of relational, pastoral, or redemptive practices—but in the concrete teachings on solidarity and enactments of reconciliation in which real flesh and blood is redeemed and restored to dignity. How might *Nostra Aetate* serve the world of human encounter and relationship as a whole, not merely the concerns of Christian doctrine vis-à-vis other religious ways? Metz reflects on his own similar pivot in this direction:

> How can one, in the face of this history of suffering, blithely ask only about one's own salvation? Early on I recognized that whoever talks of God the way Jesus does accepts the violation of preconceived religious certainty by the horrendous tragedy of others.[5]

Where we encounter religious neighbors engaged in genuine wound repair and in the redemption of living, fractured persons, there we encounter rays of divine truth. It is there that the true and the good are disclosed and performed precisely as mercy. In this way, the category "ray of divine truth" no longer functions like a projection or an a priori compliment paid to the religious neighbor, however well intended, but as a theological judgment contingent upon concrete experiences of mercy within real relationships in time and space as these relationships become scenes of transformation and redemption. Read this way, the category "ray" opens one up toward new and transformative possibilities disclosed in religious neighbors that, in turn, through dialogue can empower fresh readings and performances of mercy within one's home tradition. Where in relationships of dialogue we encounter mercy, there we encounter "rays" of divine truth.

AGAINST WOODEN READINGS OF *NOSTRA AETATE*

The sensitivities to which political theology is alive and responsive help us to avoid a wooden reading of the declaration. Promulgated near the close of the Council in 1965, *Nostra Aetate* speaks optimistically in section 1—we might ask if *too* optimistically—of humankind now being drawn closer together, of ties between people becoming stronger, about the church's task of promoting unity, love, and fellowship among people. Several theological claims are made in section 1 that specify the communitarian vocation of the human family or, in the words of Pope Francis, "a caravan of solidarity" (*Evangelii Gaudium* 87). Paragraph one affirms that humanity is *one*; that all persons as creatures of God have a shared origin in the one God and a shared end or goal (*telos*) of return to communion in the one God, who is their final cause; and that in the interim the saving design or providence of the one God extends to all persons.

Not to be overlooked is the searching anthropology the document operates with: all persons, Christian and otherwise, share a human nature that asks ultimate questions about the meaning of life, death, and suffering, of the mystery that encompasses all, with the ecclesial corollary that the church is a pilgrim people: strange, missioned, set out, but not arrived. This language constitutes the foundation on which rests all else that *Nostra Aetate* articulates, a foundation comprised by the fundamental dignity of human persons pitched into a universal framework of human identity and meaning around which real and intractable questions frame human living. According to the declaration, some of those intractable questions pertain to the "origin" and "purpose" of suffering (*Nostra Aetate* 1).

While the declaration stops short of stressing that Christians should learn techniques for understanding and addressing suffering from other religions, fifty years on it is now quite possible and appropriate to stress this very focus in connection with the activities of "dialogue" and "collaboration" with religious neighbors that the declaration does stress. *Nostra Aetate* was a beginning—not a full flowering—of dialogue. The Council fathers sought to provoke a new era of dialogue and a new way of being church by citing a few suggestive possibilities. While the human experience of suffering was one of those suggestive possibilities that received passing mention, we can direct more sustained attention to suffering and mercy as a subject of interreligious dialogue fifty years on, in a way analogous to what Metz achieved for theology as a whole by claiming, for example, that persons exercise a claim on the attention of theologians and that, in particular, suffering exercises an authoritative claim on our attention.[6] In this way, an orientation toward political theology and a conscious acceptance of the authority of suffering can protect us from wooden readings of the declaration—that dialogue is merely about ideas or doctrines or principles disconnected from the shape and fate of real lives in history—in favor of readings of the declaration that favor a constructive articulation of solidarity and mercy for a broken world. The crafts of theology and dialogue transpire in this world and no other.

In the wake of this declaration, promulgated in 1965, we can think of interreligious dialogues and experiments in comparative theology as the growing end of the declaration's reverence of elements of truth and goodness disclosed in other religious paths. Mercy captures the incarnate human experience of what it would be like to experience "truth" and "goodness" in a broken world where suffering is ubiquitous and mercy is redemptive (see *Nostra Aetate* 2). Interreligious dialogues and experiments in comparative theology, we have seen, disclose possibilities of deeper understanding and collaborative redemptive practices across religious difference that may not otherwise have been detected absent encounter. Comparative theology in this key becomes sensitive and responsive to human suffering as a theological question so that, according to the metaphor of Metz, we "face the world" to encounter it as it is, a world of persons marked by indescribable dignity while also confronted by crippling inequality, victimization, and brokenness. Theological reflection undertaken amid this world, that is, in the presence of these persons and as a form of response to them, attunes to brokenness in all its variations and addresses therapeutically those who suffer denigration as well as those who denigrate, conscious, once more, of the solidarity for which all are intended (see *Nostra Aetate* 1). Theological reflection undertaken amid this world attunes to new learnings and fresh performances of mercy enabled through dialogue with religious neighbors.

A wooden reading of *Nostra Aetate*'s conciliatory statements of theological inclusion in section 2 would rest content with an abstract or tacit supposition that others' religious traditions and teachings may contain a ray of the truth of which Christ, in his fullness, reveals in plenary form. As a preliminary but not sufficient step in interreligious dialogue, this move might become instrumental in enabling dialogue and learning across boundaries infrequently crossed during the history of the church. But a tacit or abstract supposition of others' truth need not give rise to such learning. Indeed, with the inclusive supposition in place, one might rest content not to explore it or even test it.[7] This form of inclusion, however formally correct and well-intentioned, learns little because it remains abstract, untested, and ultimately can offer no meaningful response to the world of suffering persons, a world which, on the one hand, is difficult to look at and thus frequently isn't looked at as a theological question and, on the other, is nevertheless the proper object of theological reflection and of pastoral care. Metz names the temptation we all face:

> [Political] theology works against the constant tendency of all religious worldviews to mythically camouflage the horrific disasters in the world and also works against a speculative retouching and an idealistic smoothing out of the actual course of history in order finally to make the victims invisible and their screams inaudible.[8]

A wooden reading of *Nostra Aetate* rests content with abstract formulations of truth and goodness in religious teachings and traditions, possibly overlooking the declaration's focal first paragraph pertaining to interpersonal unity and the solidarity of the human family flouted in every act of violence or disintegration. But to take seriously the vocation to unity in section 1, the problematic contexts of living and dying in which persons find themselves require attention and, where attention is lacking, strategies of interruption. Given the broader context of brokenness imbedded not only in persons but also in their time and place, the "rays of divine truth" articulated in section 2 take on the clear urgency of responding to a problem driven deep into the human condition, to which redemptive practices could then be announced and offered up strategically. The truth in which other's religious traditions participate, and of which Christ is said to be the plenary expression, is a truth that envisions a fullness and completeness of human life and flourishing as the goal for which persons were created and as the specific way Christ relates to them as their end or goal (*telos*). Where life is then fractured, ignored, snuffed out, or deprived of dignity, the category of truth in *Nostra Aetate* 2 cannot refer merely to propositions or even doctrines however gracefully articulated, or to great exchanges of ideas and thought projects.

The category of truth must, in hope, refer to concrete redemptive promises and practices that reconcile persons one to another and testify, in this world, to their fundamental dignity by recovering it from conditions that threaten. This is not to impose an alien framework of mercy onto *Nostra Aetate*, but to recover a deeply imbedded meaning already present in the Council's declaration retrieved through conversation with Metz's political theology. Operating with this vision of truth is to submit meaningfully to the personal self-interrogation Metz modeled in 1992, on the 500th anniversary of Christopher Columbus sailing to the "new world," which was the world inhabited already by Native peoples of North and South America. The 500th anniversary of that event—a catastrophe for untold many—became an occasion for Metz to wonder whether Christians in Europe "bear to look at these faces? Can we, do we want to, risk the change of perspective and see ourselves as Christians, in the churches—at least for a moment—from the perspective of these faces."[9] Or do we define ourselves with our backs to these faces? Metz continues, "Once again, the faces, and even more the eyes. With what eyes was Latin America, was this 'Catholic continent,' discovered?"[10] Those engaged in practices of comparative theology or interreligious dialogue do well to level a similar inquiry toward their own disciplines and roles within them: attitudes of inclusion often shelter blind spots or exclusions, and Metz's antidote of "interruption" responds precisely to these forms of ignorance, self-justification, and partiality imbedded deeply in the human condition.[11]

RECEPTIONS

The remainder of this essay offers three brief explorations of ways in which Catholic theology might engage in a dialogue over redemptive practices. This dialogue will be with two prominent North American religious teachers, Orthodox Jewish Rabbi Irving Greenberg and Tibetan Buddhist Lama and Prof. John Makransky, both of whom seriously engage Christian theology in dialogue and are alive to an orientation in "political theology" even if they do not self-identify as such.

Reception #1: Inviolable Dignity and Subjectivity Specify Human Persons Theologically

Distinguished North American Rabbi Irving Greenberg construes the Jewish category of "covenant" as the scene where persons participate in covenantal practices whereby life is chosen over death and maximized. Greenberg intones a no-nonsense, post-Shoah, sober recognition that some of us in the contemporary world have underestimated evil at great cost. A theology of the *imago Dei* can respond at least in part by registering three fundamental and interactive dignities. He draws from both the Jerusalem Talmud and Babylonian Talmud, to argue, first, that an image of God possesses *infinite value*. To save one such life is to have saved an infinity, since an image of God that has infinite value is different in kind from the images created by men and women—even the paintings of van Gogh, he cites by way of example—that hold but finite value.

Second, images of God are *equal*. Whereas a four-year old daughter's daily paintings at school may be assessed as less valuable than a van Gogh painting, no infinitely valuable image of God can be preferred over another. From a theological perspective, the human person as image of God admits of no rank, hierarchy, or preferential status. All images of God are equal; to think and behave otherwise is to counsel idolatry, a category Greenberg and others rightly invoke beyond the conventional scope of a faulty God relation.

Idolatry is a being/force/faith/weltanschauung that is, in its condition, partial and fragmentary; in some cases in its partial state it is a source of good. But in its idolatrous form it assumes the guise of being whole and unlimited—thereby it becomes unlimitedly evil.[12]

Third, the test of whether we see each other as images of God is whether we see each other as *unique*. Here Greenberg imbeds human diversity into unity itself, expresses the irreducible subjectivity of human persons, and calls for nonhegemonic patterns of relating.

These interactive dignities stemming from creation in the image and likeness of God have consequences for Greenberg's theology of religious pluralism. The opportunity of Jews to engage or partner with non-Jews enables them to recognize they were brought into being mutually by the love of God, and for the purpose of sharing with God—as an image of God—the divine task of repairing and healing the world (*tikkun olam*). This becomes not only a principle governing a theology of religious pluralism, but a shorthand for what the covenant must be from a Jewish perspective.

The primary criterion of judgment, then, is [the religions']
effectiveness in advancing *tikkun olam*—not their superiority as a recipient of revelation or their theological rightness
vis-à-vis others….In willing partnership, they must make
urgent cause with each other and with every faith or force
willing to advance *tikkun olam*.[13]

Likewise, John Makransky seeks to retrieve Tibetan Buddhist teachings and articulate them in fresh, empowering ways, in order to express and act upon the dignity of personhood precisely where this is denied. Makransky is a scholar of Tibetan Buddhism and comparative theology at Boston College who also serves as an ordained Lama and as cofounder of two socially engaged, contemplative organizations.[14] His tradition stresses Buddha-nature (*tathagatagarbha*) as the unconditioned primal goodness immutably inherent in all beings as seed, embryo, or kernel. Buddha-nature is thus the very ground of all experience, equally when victims are suppressed and unacknowledged as when perpetrators are suppressing and concealing, and both sets of persons are viewed with purified perception according to the bound-

less attitudes of love, compassion, joy, and equanimity. These boundless attitudes are innate capacities of mind and can be accessed through
meditation practices.[15]

In all cases, the unconditioned Buddha-nature perceives, but in
distorting ways that reflect the mind's superimposition of ignorance,
or, alternatively, the mind's purified perception, as well as a range of
possibilities in between. Consequently, Makransky retrieves contemplative practices of meditation that access the unconditioned truth
lying within oneself and equally within all beings. He retrieves and
adapts ancient Tibetan Buddhist mind training to generate a discipline
or practice whereby one can recognize and engage one's own forms of
ignorance and work out the implications of such self-perception for
recognition and honoring of the Buddha-nature deep within all living
beings known and unknown, friendly and unfriendly.

Makransky adapts meditation techniques to a contemporary audience, and in so doing enables them—whether Buddhist or not—to
purify their own self-image by recalling benefactors who have wished
one deepest well-being and love, and who have resonated with or
reflected one's own Buddha-nature precisely by offering unconditional
positive regard or love. While only the first of four steps, this prescrip-
tive spiritual practice enables one to commune with one's own primor-
dial goodness or Buddha-nature—which is the unconditioned capacity
for unrestricted love—by being shown, through a benefactor or spiritual mentor, one's own profound lovability.[16] In this way, meditation
can become a profound spiritual practice through which a teaching
mentor can communicate possibilities of mercy to a student who can,
through the same practice, adopt the same attitudes of mercy toward
herself that her mentor modeled and that also happen to align with and
express her own Buddha-nature (*tathagatagarbha*).

Reception #2: Redemption Requires Ideology Critique

Makransky's motivation to stress the primal goodness of the
ground of all being (*Buddha-nature*) opposes our tendency to reify our
own common experience of the opposite, namely, partiality, prejudice, and narrow self-interest, which create fear-based interpersonal
patterns of relating that heap victim upon victim. For as optimistic as
his Buddha-nature theological anthropology might appear, it is equally
serious about the broken state into which we have all been conditioned

and reified, and that covers over the primal goodness of each living being as Buddha-nature. The category of karma here refers not merely to personal patterns of acting and reacting that extend consequence into the future in an unpredictable way, as serious and consequential as these are; it refers analogously to social patterns of framing and naming reality, self, and others that exercise a conditioning influence over individuals and their capacity to perceive the unconditioned truth within conditioned experience.[17] His Buddhist tradition labels this condition "cyclic existence" or samsara, the state of conventional perception wherein we are conditioned by others and in turn condition each other to perceive the primal goodness of others through the narrow concerns of a brittle and reified self, given over to partiality, fear, and divisiveness. The boundless attitudes of love, compassion, joy, and equanimity remain obscured from the very beings for whom these attitudes are most foundational and basic (even when obscured).

Against this trend, the Buddhist tradition speaks of the boundless attitude of equanimity as a purified perception that begins with self (as intrinsically lovable) and radiates the same purified perception toward others, progressively: first, toward dear loved ones; then, friends, strangers, and enemies, successively. Such purified perception spontaneously perceives these various others fundamentally as lovable and wishes them deepest freedom from suffering and its causes. Such perception becomes possible as opposed to laughable through an intensive spiritual practice bearing potential to transform oneself and others precisely because the construction of "self" and "other" is shown to be *conventional*, not ultimate. Very sensibly, the transformation of social structures hinges first on the individual's own purified perception, such that any enactment toward others of the boundless attitudes of love, compassion, joy, and equanimity effects in others the change that first occurred in oneself, by disclosing it as most real. In this way, genuine transformation is possible, personally unique, and can be learned through modeling and the commitment to a personal practice or discipline. But one is not to be naïve about the unconscious nature and durability of ideologies that would thwart purified perception. Makransky discusses in detail the extent to which much of our personal and collective mental life is caught in a cyclic pattern of action and reaction to false realities mistaken as objective and true, heaping painful reaction upon reaction until we can scarcely discern the difference between pure and impure perception.[18]

Irving Greenberg, likewise, expresses an acute interest in retarding prejudice, sharing Makransky's judgment that processes of "othering" condition communities toward violence. At a conference titled *Beyond Violence: Religious Sources for Social Transformation* (2003), Rabbi Greenberg articulated how Jews might retain the particularity of Jewish faith and life even while embracing attitudes of pluralism and self-criticism that lessen the desecration of God's name (*chillul hashem*). "At the heart of the world," he writes, "is a crack; reality is fundamentally flawed."[19] The holocaust disclosed this crack in an unprecedented manner, so that with the holocaust, according to Greenberg, Jewish notions of covenant and redemption have likewise been broken. Greenberg is known for the rather thought-provoking claim that in the unfathomable wake of the *Shoah*, no theological statement should be tendered that would not be credible in the presence of burning children. For Greenberg, the *Shoah* demonstrated that God is more hidden than the rabbis previously believed, such that the Jewish people have become the "senior partner" in the covenantal enterprise. "God now acts primarily, at least on the visible level, through human activity."[20] This seriousness of purpose and willingness to take responsibility in this way for the world leads Greenberg to conclude that the religious attitude of "pluralism" functions like a prophylactic against absolutism. Pluralism enables one to restore the image of God in every person. It exposes the presumption of one's own wholeness or self-sufficiency. The lack of questioning, self-criticism, and openness to different and opposing visions is inauthentic and prone to a revolving door of absolutisms or idolatries that, inevitably, manufacture and denigrate an out-group by associating the group with a universal negative stereotype. For the in-group, of course, the stereotype has a group-binding effect, but at the cost of replacing sensitivity and affect with contempt. Greenberg writes,

> The holocaust has unleashed a paroxysm of Christian self-critique and theological determination to overcome the "teaching of contempt" tradition....Of course, the Shoah has also dramatized the moral outrageousness of any tradition's—and that includes Judaism's—carrying on unrevised, negative stereotypes or contemptuous judgments that degrade the other. Contempt breeds apathy to others' fate, if not the will to participate in assault upon them. "Never

again" demands the end of *all* contempt traditions wherever located, at all cost and as swiftly as possible.[21]

Reception #3: Religious Particularities Pose No Scandal and May Be Embraced in Nonoppositional Ways

Greenberg's use of the term *pluralism* should not be conflated with use of that term as a technical category in the context of debates over Christian theologies of religious pluralism. In those debates, some regard pluralism to be relativism. That assumption is as problematic for advocates of Christian pluralism as it is as a description of Greenberg's project. Nor does Greenberg employ pluralism as a corrective to inclusivism generally or the inclusivism of *Nostra Aetate* 2 specifically, which he never interacts with in writing despite his significant engagement with the declaration's fourth paragraph on relations with the Jewish people.

Rather, Greenberg's advocacy of pluralism defends and celebrates the particularity of "covenant" construed as the conviction that God acts in distinctive ways toward distinctive people. Because "absolutism" is a ubiquitous human vulnerability, Greenberg calls for particular covenants to be refreshed through dialogue with other particular covenants. In this way, covenants are authentic to the degree that they engage in *tikkun olam*: the enterprise of wound repair, redemption, and perfection of the world for which God has invited all covenanting people to live and work.

Suggestive of future work to be done, the category "rays of divine truth" in *Nostra Aetate* 2 functions powerfully. It rests upon a pastorally sensitive vocation to human unity (*Nostra Aetate* 1) that directs us to learn from others how best to face the many worlds of human suffering—through acknowledgment and repair—with meaningful praxis and patient commitment discovered and deepened interactively through relationship. In this sense, "rays of divine truth" signals much more than a tacit but unexplored commitment to a predetermined gradient of truth in other people's religions. An honest particularism is one that recognizes others not despite but because of one's own narratives of meaning. Many acknowledge that *Nostra Aetate* marked a beginning—not culmination—of interreligious dialogue for the Catholic Church. We continue in the tradition by building the tradition not by tacit and abstract statements about truth in other religions, but by developing the scope and practical learning given to the church as an opportunity in *Nostra Aetate*. This opportunity posed by dialogue has Christians *facing* our religious neighbors, and in three ways.

First, the interplay of Metz's political theology with Irving Greenberg and John Makransky suggests we must face neighbors by engaging meaningfully in *dialogue with a view to listening and receiving and not merely speaking*. By listening and receiving—not merely speaking—we discover an important dimension of mercy, namely, the humanization of persons. That is, our neighbors have faces, each one a portal into an entire world for those willing and ready to gaze. Facing them in this sense moves decidedly away from an abstract or a priori theology of *religions*, however inclusive and well-intentioned, toward concrete interpersonal encounter between *persons* of religious difference, each an entire world unto him- or herself and each, in irreducibly personal ways, negotiating religious identity amid their time and place at the granular level of history. Facing our neighbors in this first sense might require listening and receiving and not merely speaking to learn fresh meanings and performances of the truth—rays of divine truth—outside of Christian experience.

Facing religious neighbors in a second sense renders *the theological task primarily an intimate interpersonal encounter oriented toward binding the wounds of history* and alive to collaborative practices of harm prevention. For Greenberg, the performance of Jewish and of other covenants requires *tikkun olam*—wound repair, perfection, or redemption. For Makransky, the Buddha-nature latent deep within all living beings requires disciplines and practices that render beings transparent to their own ground of being or Buddha-nature. Both *tikkun olam* and Buddhist meditative disciplines around loving-kindness, compassion, and equanimity function as forms of interpersonal encounter that bind the wounds of individuals and of histories. They enact mercy by naming and altering the false and injurious presuppositions about self and other persons. For Metz, facing our neighbors in this second sense is mandated by the creed itself, especially the phrase "suffered under Pontius Pilate," which refers us in the first instance to a person in a specific time and place whose cross reveals powerfully the nature and scope of suffering for all, as well as the promise of being redeemed, pulled back, or reclaimed from that which threatens. In the presence of the cross, theology becomes an I-Thou encounter between persons of religious commitment who recognize in each other "the sacred grandeur of the neighbor," even to the point of giving voice to those strange differences that render each person distinctive, unique, but no less valuable than the other, as images of God or, in Makransky's Buddhist framework, Buddha-nature.[22] Where dialogues or encounters between persons render them transparent to one another's human dignity and deepest truth, however defined and understood in specific religious terms, there we encounter rays of divine truth—or mercy.

Third, facing our religious neighbors requires *prophetic courage* to name and deny those systems that threaten, violate, and harm persons by silencing them, removing them from sight, or by projecting onto their faces false identities or stereotypes that denigrate and distort. This third sense of facing our neighbors requires the critical imagination and courage needed to deny the lie told by systems of power by interrupting those systems, even at personal cost. It requires the prophetic telling and retelling of the truth concerning what Greenberg refers to as the inviolable dignity, uniqueness, and equality of all, or what Makransky refers to as the unconditioned Buddha-nature, lovability, and desire of all to be free from suffering and its causes. This third sense of facing our religious neighbors reveals an additional dimension to the meaning of mercy, namely, the attitude that oppressive systems and persons must be approached with a view to their possible transformation toward a wholeness or goodness they do not currently value but that can be opened through dialogue as a new horizon of human possibility.

With their companions in dialogue, Christians can reinterpret and refresh their own central documents and traditions. This essay has explored the well-known language in *Nostra Aetate* affirming other religious paths as containing "rays of divine truth." The Council fathers used that language as a formal term intended to pay compliment and express solidarity with those traditions, without specifying material content to the truth imputed in those traditions. What would it be like for Christians to look to their neighbors to provide material content to such "truth"? What would it be like if Metz's political theology were to provide the agenda? A new era of dialogue could emerge, animated both by a sober recognition of the situations in which persons live, suffer, and die, and by a commitment to recast theological investigation and speech in terms of a fuller range of redemptive possibilities made available through dialogue.

NOTES

1. Walter Kasper, "Open House: How Pope Francis Sees the Church," *Commonweal* (April 10, 2015): 15.

2. See http://w2.vatican.va/content/francesco/en/apost_exhorta tions/documents/papa-francesco_esortazione-ap_20131124_evangelii -gaudium.html.

3. See http://www.vatican.va/archive/hist_councils/ii_vatican _council/documents/vat-ii_decl_19651028_nostra-aetate_en.html.

4. Johann Baptist Metz, "In the Pluralism of Religious and Cultural Worlds: Notes toward a Theological and Political Program," *Cross Currents* (Summer 1999): 233.

5. Johann Baptist Metz, "Facing the World: A Theological and Biographical Inquiry," *Theological Studies* 75, no. 1 (2014): 27.

6. See, e.g., Johann Baptist Metz, "Under the Spell of Cultural Amnesia?" in *Missing God? Cultural Amnesia and Political Theology*, ed. John K. Downey, Jürgen Manemann, and Steven T. Ostovich (Berlin: Lit Verlag, 2006), 10.

7. Francis Cardinal Arinze, "The Role of the Catholic University in the Promotion of Interreligious Dialogue," *Louvain Studies* 23 (1998): 307–20.

8. Metz, "Facing the World," 26–27.

9. Johann Baptist Metz, "1492—Through the Eyes of a European Theologian," in this volume, page 10.

10. Ibid., 12.

11. This tension is revealed in the genesis of *Nostra Aetate* itself, with its disagreements among the drafters over years regarding the relationship between the church's classical heritage and the motivation to revise its dysfunctional relationship with Judaism and the Jewish people. "The understandable result," comments Greenberg, "was *Nostra Aetate*, section four, an admixture of elements out of the rethinking, tolerance, and traditional models." Irving Greenberg, "New Revelations and New Patterns in the Relationship of Judaism and Christianity," *Journal of Ecumenical Studies* 16, no. 2 (1979): 253.

12. Irving Greenberg, "Theology after the Shoah: The Transformation of the Core Paradigm," *Modern Judaism* 26, no. 2 (2006): 218.

13. Irving Greenberg, "To Repair the World: Judaism and Christianity in Partnership," *Review and Expositor* 103 (2006): 165.

14. See http://courageofcare.org/.

15. John Makransky, "No Real Protection without Authentic Love and Compassion," *Journal of Buddhist Ethics* 12 (2005): 25–26.

16. John Makransky, *Awakening through Love* (Boston: Wisdom Publications, 2007), 15–32.

17. Ibid., 106; John N. Sheveland, "Review of *Awakening through Love*," *Journal of Buddhist Ethics* 15 (2008): 31–39.

18. Makransky, *Awakening through Love*, 108.

19. Michael Oppenheim, "Irving Greenberg and a Jewish Dialectic of Hope," *Judaism* (2000): 197.

20. Irving Greenberg, *Living in the Image of God: Jewish Teachings to Perfect the World* (Northvale, NJ: Jason Aronson, 1998), 38, as cited in Oppenheim, "Irving Greenberg and a Jewish Dialectic of Hope," 195.

21. Irving Greenberg, "Covenantal Pluralism," *Journal of Ecumenical Studies* 34, no. 3 (1997): 432.

22. Metz, "1492," 12; Pope Francis, *Evangelii Gaudium*, no. 92.

8

"Howling Over the Sins in Which We Share"

Dorothy Day and Racial Mercy

Maureen O'Connell

In his address to the U.S. Congress in September 2015, just weeks before opening the Jubilee Year of Mercy, Pope Francis remembered Abraham Lincoln, Martin Luther King, Dorothy Day, and Thomas Merton as figures of American history who "shaped the fundamental values" of the United States and as such "offer a way of seeing and interpreting reality." Francis said of Dorothy Day, "In these times when social concerns are so important, I cannot fail to mention the Servant of God Dorothy Day, who founded the Catholic Worker Movement. Her social activism, her passion for justice and for the cause of the oppressed, were inspired by the Gospel, her faith, and the example of the saints."[1]

Day (1897–1980), long lifted up as an icon of American Catholicism, confounds the usual dichotomies fueling the generative tensions in the American church.[2] Her many biographers suggest she would resist the evolving cause for her sainthood if it were up to her. Francis noted that Day lived her discipleship amid financial crisis and economic hardship and with a heart and mind attuned to those "trapped in the cycle of poverty." He remembered Day as one who witnessed to a fundamental conviction of the Christian faith that "the fight against poverty and hunger must be fought constantly and on many fronts, *especially in its causes*."[3]

If racism is indeed a root cause of "the cycle of poverty"[4] and our "economy of exclusion" in the United States (*Evangelii Gaudium* 53–54),[5] then American Catholics need to turn and face the persistent legacy of racism in our country and in our church. Although a relatively unexplored facet of her prophetic ministry, Day offers an example of an American disciple who deliberately turned to face the suffering of racism, whether in northern urban centers or rural southern towns. In 1943, in her *Catholic Worker* column, "On Pilgrimage," Dorothy Day reflected on her visits to black communities in Paterson, NJ, and in the Deep South, where she heard narratives of the anguish of racial violence:

> Are not these sins crying to heaven for vengeance? And how can we do anything but howl over the sins in which we share? They are our sins. Just as we believe in the communion of saints—that we share in the merits of the saints, so we must believe that we share in the guilt of such cruelty and injustice.[6]

These four sentences reflect Johann Baptist Metz's fundamental claim that "[Christianity] is mystical and political at the same time and it leads us into a responsibility, not only for what we fail to do but also for what we allow to happen to others in our presence, before our eyes."[7] In some ways, Day's reflections on the Great Migration era North and Jim Crow era South predate Metz's observations of postholocaust Germany. She laments that if Christianity could not howl over the sins of racism, then Christianity, to use Metz's language, "does not live discipleship but only believes in discipleship and, under the cover of merely believed-in discipleship, goes its own way."[8]

I want to "remembrance" Dorothy Day, to remember her in the liturgical sense of this word or as to become more like that which we remember, as someone who worked in her own time to probe and heal the wounds of racism in her white self, her predominantly white Catholic Church, and our American culture of white supremacy. I contend that we must remembrance her in "the skin she was in"—as a white, lay, Catholic woman, mother, and grandmother—who implicitly and explicitly worked to dismantle white supremacy at the heart of America's "racial contract" that has structured U.S. culture since the arrival of Europeans on the continent.[9] While acknowledging the caveats of a white scholar centering discussions of racism on the experience of yet another white person, I will highlight how Day offers *de-centering* alternatives to white approaches to racial justice work. In the process, I will develop the concept of "racial mercy," a phrase she never used but that was evident in her engagement with what W. E. B. DuBois called, at the turn of the century in which Day would live her discipleship, the "color line." By racial mercy, I mean the capability to name and probe the wounds of racism, acknowledge privately and publicly our failures, and in the same manner, seek forgiveness and start again.

In short, Day helps us to see that racial mercy echoes a central imperative of Metzian political theology, namely that the transformation of social reality depends on the willingness and capability of those with their backs turned to suffering—that of others and their own—to become more fully human.[10] I'll make this case in three steps. First, using the framework of political theology, I will explain why I think American Catholics, particularly white Catholics, need to step back from our commitments to racial *justice* and ponder instead the more fundamental call to racial *mercy* in order to interrupt the bourgeois Christianity of our time, namely white supremacy. Second, culling notions of mercy from Metzian political theology, I will propose Dorothy Day as an exemplar of racial mercy. I will conclude by pointing out how Day's life illuminates the political possibilities, in the Metzian sense of the word, of racial mercy for reshaping white Catholics' approaches to racism.

BOURGEOIS CHRISTIANITY AND THE UPPER ROOM OF WHITE SUPREMACY

The more I understand racism from the perspective of white supremacy, which created and sustains trauma inducing skin-identity hierarchies in the name of socioeconomic power, the more Metz's compelling notion of bourgeois Christianity—which enabled German Christians to practice a "believed-in discipleship" or an "untroubled

believing and praying with [their] backs turned to Auschwitz"[11]—
interrupts Christian understandings of racism in the United States.
Metz is troubled by the "relatively large degree of harmony between
the practice of religion and the experience of life within society,"[12] what
he calls a "bourgeois Christianity" that supports the notion of a privatized and invulnerable God distant from and unmoved by human suffering at the hands of others, and therefore responsible for it. Bourgeois
Christianity sustains an anthropology of domination built on dualism
and the invisibility of suffering and demands lack of empathy in order
to sustain a false sense of moral goodness and innocence.

Connections between bourgeois Christianity and white supremacy abound. By white supremacy, I mean the beliefs, dispositions, and
behaviors that reflect and defend the superiority and normativity of
the white experience;[13] justify continued racial inequality by assessing
people of color as culturally or morally deficient;[14] motivate weak commitments to racial justice by "disremembering the past" and appealing to inflated notions of white innocence and moral goodness;[15] and
shape encounters with racially different others with the twin responses
of fear and guilt.[16] Eddie Glaude suggests, "White supremacy involves
the way a society organizes itself, and what and whom it chooses to
value." Whether Nazi Germany or apartheid South Africa, the era of
Jim Crowe or hyperincarceration, Glaude notes that white supremacy
gives rise to a set of beliefs and practices "informed by the fundamental belief that white people are more valuable than others."[17] Since
its inception in the United States, white supremacy has created what
he calls a "value gap" that has brought devastation to communities of
color, whose protests whites have only ever met, at best, with indifference but often with violent rejection. In a way that echoes Metz's
concerns about the threats a "believed-in" faith poses to Christianity,
Glaude suggests that an easy partnership between the value gap of white
supremacy and the "American Idea" is destroying our democracy: "If
you believe that white people matter more than black people, then the
principles of freedom, liberty, and equality—democracy itself—will be
distorted and disfigured."[18]

Perhaps more troubling, however, is the fact that white supremacy in the United States is also anchored in a distorted Christianity.
Kelly Brown Douglas identifies a "racial-religious synchronicity" at the
heart of the myth of American exceptionalism that created and sustains
white supremacy by constructing Christian whiteness in opposition to

blackness: "To be a chosen nation is to be an Anglo-Saxon nation, to be an Anglo-Saxon nation is to be a chosen nation."[19] Joseph Barndt suggests Christianity "midwifed" racism primarily through the worship of the God of the "Rulers' Church," personified with the traits and virtues of the mythical Anglo-Saxons: power, sovereignty, and conquest.[20] As a result, Mary Elizabeth Hobgood claims that individual and collective drive to white dominance necessitates an inability of whites for self-love, since in order to maintain racial hierarchies, whites constantly need to deny fundamental things about our own humanity in order to justify dehumanizing others.[21] And if white culture is built on "presumptions of dominance and entitlement," as Bryan Massingale suggests, then white Catholics experience our whiteness in terms of walls that separate us from the rest of the Body of Christ: walls of ignorance, fear, mistrust, and denial.[22] In many ways, these theological investigations of white supremacy echo two of Metz's fundamental conclusions about the dangers of bourgeois Christianity: "Man [*sic*] is by subjugating,"[23] and "all too pervasively is our bourgeois Christianity founded on invisibility, on noninterference, on non-touching, on dualism. And we have long become masters in the art of making invisible."[24]

When "under the cloak" of white supremacy, Christianity in the United States is akin to the experience of the disciples in the upper room after the crucifixion and yet before the appearance of the risen Jesus, a space of longing for an infusion of mercy. White Catholics in the United States are walled off from the reconciling joy of the resurrection because we haven't faced our collective complicity in the crucifixion of people of color in our history and in our midst. We are paralyzed by our unquestioned confidence in what we think we know about racism in the echo chamber of our white-only conversations or predominately white academies and boardrooms, high schools and universities, churches and governments. We are stuck in a mental space where we reject the need for healing out of fear of those whom we've harmed. We are hamstrung by our amnesia where the memory of Jesus's acts of love of the neighbor and forgiveness of sinners is concerned, and we are caught in the repetitive loop of history to which we are responding, at best, with inequality-sustaining charity. We are blinded by our own judgments about the people on the receiving end of our charity, and anesthetized by our self-righteous anger when they are not sufficiently grateful. We are burdened by gifts we often don't even know we have and clueless as to how to contribute to movements of inclusion. We are choosing self-isolation in the suffocating anxiety of an all-white upper room of our own making rather than encountering the liberating mercy of the wounded and yet resurrected Christ in the people outside the door.

Perhaps most problematic, being stuck in this upper room of whiteness hinders the work we do toward bridging, blurring, or erasing the color line, which is what justice demands. Just as Metz insisted that a bourgeois Christianity was incapable of turning and facing the suffering of Auschwitz, its counterpart in contemporary American Christianity renders attempts at racial justice, even on the part of Christians, inadequate. By protecting us from pain, the upper room reinforces within us a sense of justice as pragmatic where racism is concerned: that we can somehow "fix this race thing" without having to rend our hearts wide open by coming face-to-face with anyone it harms, or without turning to face the history of racial hate and discrimination in our families or our churches. Instead, the upper room of whiteness falsely assures us that we can build the kingdom of God without having, in the words of liberation theologian Roberto Goizueta, to experience the wounded resurrection by probing the wounds of the resurrected Christ.[25] Without that knowledge, justice misses the subtle and yet weighty nuances of racism that wound the Body of Christ today—nuances that sustain inequality built into systems and structures and that reside in hearts. Moreover, by sustaining racial segregation that precludes encounters with difference, the upper room gives us the false sense that white ways really are the best ways, that white knowledge really is the most comprehensive, that white analysis—or at least information run through white filters—is the most accurate and trustworthy in the end. In the upper room, justice takes on the trappings of the Enlightenment, one of the intellectual wellsprings of the very concept of race. Justice is a kind of moral calculus, a logical proposition, a set of theories and hypotheticals pondered and parsed, rooted in authority insured by hierarchy, intoned with rhetorical fervor, and brought about through relationships of exchange. It is never fully informed by lived and multicultural realities on the other side of the locked door, and so rings empty and false on those ears outside while continuing to support familiar strategies that fail.

By providing a closed space that incubates fear, the upper room normalizes fear and tethers justice to it, cutting off empathy and choking creativity, both of which are critical human capabilities for life in community. When tethered to fear, justice cannot incorporate "outside the box" or "green light" thinking. It is limited by questions of practicality, effectiveness, feasibility, assessable outcomes, political correctness, and security; these criteria too often overpower the gratuitousness, outrageousness, abundance, and surety of neighbor love. Finally, by locking out whatever might be on the other side, the upper room separates whites not only from our neighbors of color and their perceptions of us, but also from the vision that God has of us—a vision of us as broken and yet still deeply loved, *beloved*, people. Too often the upper room keeps our gaze turned in on ourselves, tempting us to deny our brokenness and sinfulness where racism is concerned and so to miss the wounds in need of healing, whether in our own bodies or on those of others. So justice never gets to the heart of the matter—changing the fundamental ways we understand ourselves and others. Moreover, in the upper room, whites often become so overwhelmed by our complicity in this profound woundedness that we react with paralyzing guilt and shame. Talk of justice gets derailed, either with white defensiveness or white fragility, and joins the litany of just one more "believed in" dimension of Christianity.

DOROTHY DAY AND RACIAL MERCY

Metz contends that the central antidote to bourgeois Christianity after Auschwitz is the "conversion of bourgeois hearts" from excess of power, wealth, consumerism, and apathy, a "communitarian-political process" that "can only be achieved together and with others."[26] "[The conversion of hearts] is the most radical and most challenging form of conversion and revolution," Metz claims, "and it is so because transforming situations in society never changes all that really needs to be changed."[27] The pope appears to be echoing this fundamental conviction of political theology in his Papal Bull Announcing the Jubilee Year of Mercy, where he notes the link between mercy and justice: "Mercy is not opposed to justice but rather expresses God's way of reaching out to the sinner, offering him a new chance to look at himself, convert, and believe" (*Misericordiae Vultus* 21).[28]

I suggest that before we can do racial justice, white Christians might need first to seek *racial mercy* amid the upper room of whiteness. Developing moral theologian James Keenan's definition of mercy as the virtue that enables us to enter the chaos of other people's lives,[29] I define racial mercy as the capability for white Christians in the United States to move beyond the security of the upper room and out into the dangerous chaos that sustaining white supremacy has created in our individual lives and white communities, as well as the wider community. With the help of mercy, the work of racial justice becomes a pilgrimage, a way of moving out of ourselves and our predominantly white enclaves, journeying with humility and courage to the outskirts of our emotional, intellectual, political, spiritual, or liturgical comfort zones, buoyed by the confidence promised by the God of mercy that when we get it wrong—and we do and will—that we can acknowledge it, seek forgiveness from God and others, and then try again. With racial mercy, we can, in the words of Emory philosopher George Yancy, "tarry" with our whiteness, recognizing that justice is not a destination when it comes to racism, but a way of being in the midst of the historical legacy of white domination.[30] Consider four ways Dorothy Day embodies the capability for racial mercy.

First, Day made herself vulnerable enough to notice others' pain, experience it as her own, and then go public with it. As testimony to her own gradual process of moving from being locked in the upper room of whiteness, to probing the wounds of the resurrected Christ, to heading to the chaos of the streets, her vocation evolved from that of a *socially conscious reporter* with a distanced perch to observe the social inequality and upheavals of her days, to that of a *sympathizer* who goes to jail with others and then converts to Catholicism in order to share in the experiences of the masses she observed, to that of an *empathizer* who weeps with the profound recognition of shared pain and the sufferings of the world, to that of a *lamenter* who interrupts the status quo of white dominance by joining her white voice with cries of protest coming from communities of color, to that of an *activist* who refuses to participate in the structural causes of this suffering. A willingness to become publicly vulnerable broke Day out of the bondage of her whiteness and might be the fundamental dimension of her conversion. Moreover, Day's willingness to make "visible all invisible and inconvenient suffering and—convenient or not—pay attention to it"[31] brought the dynamics of America's racial contract into sharper focus for her, a clarity that then sparked the equally radical softening of her Euro-American heart, which would have been conditioned toward hardness through a variety of Christian myths long invoked to ignore or, even worse, to justify African American suffering.[32] This softening of heart or vulnerability is essential to racial mercy since, again in Metz's words, "only when people themselves remain capable of suffering do they refrain from forcing suffering arbitrarily on others, and are able and ready in their own way to share in the sufferings of others and become active in the liberation struggles of the tortured and exploited."[33] In the context of political theology, this is called a mysticism of open eyes; in critical race theory, this is the first step toward becoming a white ally for racial justice.

While analysis of her self-described conversion experiences abound,[34] specifics of Day's own gradual process of "passing over to a new perspective on reality"[35] from that of white dominance to that of white allyship are essential for contemporary Euro-American Catholics. From the earliest days of the Catholic Worker Movement, Day knew that racism made life unnecessarily harder for some people. On Pentecost Sunday in May of 1934, she and Peter Maurin, cofounder of the movement, attended an interracial mass meeting at Town Hall in New York City, an initiative of the National Catholic Interracial Federation that worked to dismantle institutional racism within and beyond the church in areas of access to Catholic education, education for clergy, and fair housing and employment.[36] Day immediately joined the planning committee of what would become the Catholic Interracial Council in New York (CICNY), whose goal was "to promote in every practicable way, relations between the races based on Christian principles, by creating better understanding in the public as to the situation, needs, and progress of the Negro group in America through the establishment of social justice and through the practice of mutual cooperation."[37] A few months later, Day described in *The Worker* her contributions to the CICNY in terms of doing "a good deal of investigating of complaints as to churches, schools and institutions where there is said to be discrimination against the Negro and take up specific examples and try to rectify them."[38] In 1935, at the behest of a black Catholic activist in Chicago, Arthur Falls, the first African American executive secretary of the CICNY in 1963, *The Catholic Worker* changed its masthead in its second issue to include a black laborer and a white laborer reaching across the cross.

The second dimension of racial mercy in Day's life was the fact that she was no stranger to her own need for God's mercy in light of the suffering of racism, and as such her witness compels whites like her to take up the work of justice by examining conscience and culture, and by asking for forgiveness. Recall her visits to black communities in Paterson where she heard tales of racial violence: "We cannot talk of the love of God, the love of our neighbor without recognizing the dire need for penance. In a world in which such cruelty exists, in which men are so possessed, such a spirit cannot be cast out but by prayer and fasting."[39] For Day, mercy involved softening one's own heart so that ongoing critical self-reflection is possible. Mercy required courage to embrace her own shortfallings, rather than deny or resist them, and the humility to seek forgiveness constantly. Day engaged in public acts of penance that signaled both her limitations but also her willingness to try again. Fasting, protesting, marching, writing, and praying the rosary were radical acts of self-love that reminded her—and those she inspires—of our beloved status in the eyes of a merciful God.

Third, perhaps the fact that she was a woman allowed Day to see that injustice happens to "enspirited bodies," to borrow a phrase from ethicist Margaret Farley.[40] Day knew that the root of justice, therefore, requires the essential capability for empathy as well as a refusal to limit injustice to a conceptual reality but rather to understand it as a deeply embodied one: it's the headaches of hunger or the diabetes that comes with lack of access to affordable healthy food; it's the withdrawal symptoms of addiction or the depression that accompanies the trauma of violence; it's the increased levels of stress hormones when you are not able to move safely through certain spaces or the respiratory ailments that come with poor air quality. And Day also knew that injustice and poverty do something to people's spirits, to their sense of self—which can be further demoralized by acts of paternalistic charity. The works of mercy—both corporeal and spiritual—shaped the ethos of the Worker precisely because of the embodied contact they demand of all who practice them. Day's commitment to the works of mercy carries Metzian political undertones. One cannot practice the works without encountering others, without tactile meetings with embodied and enspirited suffering. Like Metz, the primary challenge of faith that this suffering presented to Day was not *why* God permits such suffering, a question that can falsely absolve us of responsibility for it, but rather *where* God is in the midst of it. Day and her compatriots believed God to be among the suffering, as Jesus explained to the disciples in the parable of the last judgment. The works of mercy, therefore, reflect

Day's "passion for God"—the God of the breadline and the God of the color line.

Moreover, as a woman, Day knew that we do justice with our bodies; as such she accepted the responsibility for seeking racial justice with her white body. She put her white body physically near other bodies that would have been considered nonwhite whether because of ethnicity, social class, skin color, or political affiliation not only in order to better empathize and understand what these enspirited bodies needed or wanted, but also to allow her white body to serve as a portal to the privileges awarded it—public attention during protests, safety during imprisonment, the sympathetic gaze of the media, and legitimacy when dealing with archbishops. And since she had a following among whites, where she went with her body would shine a spotlight on what was happening to other bodies there. Day did not shy away from the color line. In addition to the regular activities of the CICNY chapter in Harlem, which included interracial liturgies and prayer breakfasts intended to "actively challenge racial norms that contradicted Church teachings,"[41] one of her earliest trips from the Worker in New York City was at the invitation of a Southern Tenant Farmers Union, founded by Protestant ministers concerned with the plight of black tenant farmers. Decades later, she would visit the interracial community at Koinonia Farm in Americus, Georgia, during a Lenten pilgrimage where she hoped to learn from folks there about the violence of white supremacy—and she learned what it was like to be shot at during the night watch one evening. It might have been that experience that shaped her explanation toward the end of her life about what she thought the many young people who contributed to the Worker may have taken away with them: "They learn not only to love, with compassion, but to overcome fear, that dangerous emotion that precipitates violence. They may go on feeling fear, but they know the means, they have grown in faith, to overcome it."[42]

Fourth, Dorothy Day provides an exemplar of what white, nonviolent passion for justice looks like. In fact, she knew, in the words of Tim Wise, that "the power of resistance is to set an example."[43] Catholic Worker and Notre Dame ethicist Margaret Pfeil notes, "Day exhorted Catholic Worker houses of hospitality to wield the works of mercy as spiritual weapons on the frontlines of American inner cities, beginning right in their own streets" understanding that "structural transformation aligned with the revolution of values that King advocated must stand in dynamic interrelationship with personal conversion expressed in very concrete lifestyle practices."[44] When it comes to resisting white domination, Day shows us that nonviolence is an interior disposition of letting go of an identity constructed for you, which for whites means emptying ourselves of a sense of our own righteousness, our own moral goodness and innocence, a sense that we are the ones with the answers or the resources, or that our need to be forgiven trumps others' needs for justice. In emptying ourselves of these things, we are better able to enter into racial solidarity, which Massingale calls a "paschal experience" in which whites "die to a false sense of self and renunciation of racial privilege so as to rise to a new identity and status that is God-given."[45] By refusing to operate with the logic and even spirituality of whiteness, Day's life reveals that nonviolence creates a space within individuals and collectives for a new capacity for relationships.

Day's nonviolence offers evidence of what Metz calls a "militant love" akin to "treason" that betrays bourgeois virtues and discipleship, is "partisan, yet without the destructive hate which negates individual people,"[46] and is single-minded in its commitment to the ongoing conversion of one's own heart, which sparks that process in the hearts of others. Day embraces the universal quality of love that Metz describes; not a love that fails to take sides, but rather, one that, "*in the way* it takes sides, that is, without hatred or hostility toward people, even to the foolishness of the cross,"[47] is distinctively Christian. This space for new relationships is what allows alternatives to structural inequities to surface and be perceived as viable. Both require ongoing clarification of thought that can best happen when your body is drawn near to bodies closest to the pain of injustice. "For Catholic Workers, the soup line is the think tank and the seminar room," says Patrick Jordan, an editor of *Commonweal* and a former Catholic Worker. "That's where you make policy."[48]

THROWING OPEN THE DOORS OF MERCY

Dorothy Day is an American Catholic who did not approach racism through the usual dichotomy of either charity, which in addressing its ongoing effects on people misses its structural causes, or through justice, which in attending to racism's structural dimensions misses its cultural embeddedness in individual and collective psyches. Rather, we find in her an approach to resisting racism that is steeped in mercy, the healing balm for the wounds of what Bryan Massingale has publicly called the "soul sickness" of America, or what Day calls in her column back in 1943 "the sins that we all share." Pope Francis's ideas of sin in this Year of Mercy confirm the need for racial mercy: "Sin is more than a stain; sin is a wound: it needs to be treated, healed."[49] Moreover, Servant of God Dorothy Day occupies both the upper room of white supremacy and the suffering and yet redemptive world outside. She is with us whites, especially white Catholics on the inside of that locked door in that upper room of fear. And she stands among those on the other side—the farm workers organizing for better pay, the mothers fasting for fair funding for urban public schools, the incarcerated seeking rehabilitation not retribution, the college students marching to protest a militarized police, the faithful protesting the death penalty. She is one who can open wide the door of mercy, inviting whites to cross over into the messy and yet beautiful space of the wounded resurrection, inviting us to probe the wounds of the resurrected Jesus within ourselves and people around us. Racial mercy as lived by Dorothy Day reminds us of the importance of conversion in racial justice work.

Racial mercy as lived by Dorothy Day celebrates the ability to embrace our own sinfulness, to seek mercy, and to try again as a way of caring for ourselves that ethnic whites either lost or sacrificed in the process of "becoming white" in America. This self-love gives white Catholics the psychological freedom needed to acknowledge our sinfulness when it comes to racism and foster a desire for forgiveness. Forgiveness bolsters much-needed confidence to start again, turning the power dynamics at the heart of much social justice work on its head by challenging a sense of moral superiority or fear of failure. Rather than sidestepping moral failures where racism is concerned, racial mercy can undo the paralyzing bindings of rejection, denial, or voluntary ignorance that keep Euro-Americans locked up in defensive postures around our brothers and sisters of color. "If we do not begin by examining our wretchedness," Francis says in *The Church of Mercy*, "if we stay lost and despair that we will never be forgiven, we end up licking our wounds, and they stay open and never heal."[50] Much in the way that Francis is confident that mercy can transform a church that is "healthy from being confined and from clinging to its own security" into one that is "bruised, hurting and dirty,"[51] mercy might allow Euro-Americans to become, in the words of George Yancy in a *New York Times* opinion piece on the eve of the Christian Feast of the Incarnation in 2015, vulnerable or "un-sutured" or undone by the ugliness of our white supremacy in order to open ourselves to the kind of love that can change us and our racialized world.[52]

Day teaches us that racial mercy is awareness of one's body and the need for healing. When we approach justice with an eye for healing, we can more deeply appreciate that *all* people have been wounded by patriarchy and white dominance. The upper room is hardly healthy when it comes to what the dominant culture has told white Catholics about who we are, how we ought to comport our bodies, where we can go with our bodies and with whom, and what we ought to orient our lives toward. Rather than strive to be good and perfect, detached and appropriate, invulnerable and independent, in control and unemotional, Day and Francis both know that when we meditate on a God who gazes on us—sinful as we are—with love, we can be liberated from the constraints of the dominant culture and heal the wounds it has inflicted on us too. Mercy puts us back together, as individuals and as communities, by opening us to God's abundant and tender love for who we are, as individuals and diverse communities who reflect the multiplicity of God. We see in Day that racial justice might involve a way of being—a kind of racial mercy—first. Her life suggests that perhaps prioritizing pragmatism through a focus on outcomes, hard and fast solutions, has been a hindrance to racial justice all along. In his assessment of the Catholic Worker's approach to the works of mercy, American Catholic historian Jack Downey notes, "Acknowledging and confronting injustice is not itself sufficient for establishing equity, but it is a necessary, organic, first step, and ought not be suffocated simply for lack of pre-packaged systemic alternatives."[53] A frequently quoted wisdom teaching from Day popped up on Catholic social media feeds post-9/11: "No one has a right to sit down and feel hopeless. There is too much work to do."

Returning to the pope's naming of Dorothy Day as a holy American, consider Metz's reflections on the holiness of Christians who have lived "the messianic virtues of discipleship," some "at the very cost of their lives": "In these the productive model of holiness for our time shines out: holiness, not as a strictly private ideal one seeks for oneself and that could therefore easily lure one into an attitude of conformism toward the prevailing political situation but rather a holiness that proves itself in an alliance of mysticism and that militant love that draws upon itself the sufferings of others."[54] As we howl over the sins that we share and seek racial mercy, we beseech:

Servant of God, Dorothy Day—*Pray for us.*

NOTES

1. Address of the Holy Father to the Joint Session of the United States Congress, September 24, 2015, accessed January 5, 2017, https://w2.vatican.va/content/francesco/en/speeches/2015/september/documents/papa-francesco_20150924_usa-us-congress.html.

2. On this note, see Jacob Philips, "'Being Scorned by One's Own Is Perfect Joy': The Strange Case of Dorothy Day," *Journal of Religious History*, 37, no. 4 (December 2013): 528–40. Other notable biographies include Jim Forest, *All Is Grace: A Biography of Dorothy Day* (Maryknoll, NY: Orbis Books, 2011); and Paul Elie, *The Life You Save May Be Your Own: An American Pilgrimage* (New York: Farrar, Straus, and Giroux, 2004).

3. Address of the Holy Father to the Joint Session of the United States Congress, my emphasis.

4. For a thorough visual overview of the relationship between race and economic disparity in the United States, see a series of charts compiled by *The New York Times* titled, "America's Racial Divide, Charted," August 19, 2014, http://www.nytimes.com/2014/08/20/upshot/americas-racial-divide-charted.html?_r=0.

5. See https://w2.vatican.va/content/francesco/en/apost_exhortations/documents/papa-francesco_esortazione-ap_20131124_evangelii-gaudium.html.

6. Dorothy Day, "Aims and Purposes," *The Catholic Worker*, May 1943, 4, http://www.catholicworker.org/dorothyday/articles/919-plain.htm. My emphasis.

7. Johann Baptist Metz, "Christians and Jews after Auschwitz," in *Love's Strategy: The Political Theology of Johann Baptist Metz*, ed. John K. Downey (Harrisburg, PA: Trinity Press), 47.

8. Ibid.

9. Charles Mills, *The Racial Contract* (Ithaca, NY: Cornell University Press, 1999).

10. Maureen H. O'Connell, *Compassion: Loving Our Neighbor in an Age of Globalization* (Maryknoll, NY: Orbis Books, 2009), 140.

11. Metz, "Christians and Jews after Auschwitz," 47–48.

12. Johann Baptist Metz, "Messianic or Bourgeois Religion?" in *The Emergent Church: The Future of Christianity in a Postbourgeois World*, trans. Peter Mann (New York: Crossroad, 1981), 1.

13. See Peggy McIntosh's now classic "White Privilege: Unpacking the Invisible Knapsack," accessed January 5, 2017, http://code.ucsd.edu/pcosman/Backpack.pdf. See also Tim Wise, *White like Me: Reflections on Race from a Privileged Son*, rev. ed. (Berkeley, CA: Soft Skull Press, 2011).

14. Assumptions of the intellectual, moral, and cultural inferiority of people and communities of color is a central component of what Joe R. Feagin calls the "white racial frame," which he unpacks in *The White Racial Frame: Centuries of Racial Framing and Counter-Framing* (New York: Routledge, 2009).

15. On white supremacy and memory, see Eddie Glaude, *Democracy in Black: How Racism Still Enslaves the American Soul* (New York: Crown, 2016), 51–70; on moral innocence, see Barbara Applebaum, *Being White, Being Good: White Complicity, Moral Responsibility, and Social Justice Pedagogy* (Lexington, KY: Lexington Books, 2011).

16. George Yancy, *Black Bodies, White Gazes: The Continuing Significance of Race* (Lantham, MD: Rowman & Littlefield Publishers, 2008).

17. Glaude, *Democracy in Black*, 30.

18. Ibid., 34.

19. Kelly Brown Douglas, *Stand Your Ground: Black Bodies and the Justice of God* (Maryknoll, NY: Orbis Books, 2015), 16.

20. Joseph Barndt, *Becoming an Anti-Racist Church: Journeying towards Wholeness* (Minneapolis: Fortress Press, 2011), 32.

21. Mary Elizabeth Hobgood, *Dismantling Privilege: An Ethic of Accountability* (Cleveland, OH: Pilgrim Press, 2009), 48.

22. Bryan Massingale, *Racial Justice and the Catholic Church* (Maryknoll, NY: Orbis Books, 2010).

23. Johann Baptist Metz, "Bread of Survival: The Lord's Supper of Christians as Anticipatory Sign of an Anthropological Revolution," in *The Emergent Church*, 35.

24. Johann Baptist Metz, "Toward the Second Reformation," in *The Emergent Church*, 54.

25. Roberto Goizueta. *Christ Our Companion: Toward a Theological Aesthetics of Liberation* (Maryknoll, NY: Orbis Books, 2009).

26. Johann Baptist Metz, "Christianity and Politics," in *The Emergent Church*, 72.

27. Metz, "Messianic or Bourgeois Religion," 3.

28. See https://w2.vatican.va/content/francesco/en/apost_letters/documents/papa-francesco_bolla_20150411_misericordiae-vultus.html.

29. See James F. Keenan, *Jesus and Virtue Ethics: Building Bridges between New Testament Studies and Moral Theology* (New York: Sheed & Ward, 2005), 67–73; "Virtue and Identity," *Concilium* (2000/2): 69–77; and *The Works of Mercy: The Heart of Catholicism* (Lanham, MD: Rowman & Littlefield Publishers, 2007).

30. George Yancy, *Look, A White! Philosophical Essays on Whiteness* (Philadelphia: Temple University Press, 2012), 152–75.

31. Johann Baptist Metz, "A Passion for God: Religious Orders Today," in *A Passion for God: The Mystical-Political Dimension of Christianity*, trans. J. Matthew Ashley (New York: Paulist Press, 1998), 163.

32. For myths of American exceptionalism, see Douglas, *Stand Your Ground*; for the myth of the "American Dream," see Ta-Nehisi Coates, *Between the World and Me* (New York: Spiegel & Grau, 2015); for the myth of the "Ruler's Church," see Barndt, *Becoming an Anti-Racist Church*; for the myth of Christian realism, see James Cone, *The Cross and the Lynching Tree* (Maryknoll, NY: Orbis Books, 2013).

33. Metz, "The Bread of Survival," 38.

34. See Day's own account in *The Long Loneliness* (New York: Harper Brothers, 1952). See also Jim Forest, *All Is Grace*; and Paul Elie, *The Life You Save May Be Your Own*.

35. Sallie McFague, "Conversion: Life on the Edge of the Raft," *Interpretation: A Journal of the Bible and Theology* 32, no. 3 (July 1978): 255.

36. See the description of the holdings of the CICNY archives at Catholic University, accessed January 5, 2017, http://www.catholicresearch.net/vufind/Record/cuaead_0nSzie/Description#tabnav.

37. David W. Southern, *John LaFarge and the Limits of Catholic Interracialism: 1911–1963* (Baton Rouge, LA: LSU Press, 1996), 183.

38. Dorothy Day, "Day After Day," *The Catholic Worker*, July–August 1934, 4.

39. Day, "Aims and Purposes."

40. Margaret Farley, *Just Love: A Framework for Christian Sexual Ethics* (New York: Bloomsbury Academic, 2008).

41. CICNY archives at Catholic University.

42. Dorothy Day, "On Pilgrimage," *The Catholic Worker*, March/April 1975, 2 and 8, accessed January 5, 2017, http://www.catholicworker.org/dorothyday/articles/548.html.

43. Wise, *White like Me*, 74.

44. Margaret Pheil, "A Spirituality of Nonviolent White Resistance," in *The Scandal of White Complicity in US Hyper-Incarceration: A Nonviolent Spirituality of Resistance*, ed., Laurie Cassidy, Alex Mikulich, and Margaret Pfeil (New York: Palgrave MacMillan, 2013), 148.

45. Massingale, *Racial Justice and the Catholic Church*, 121.

46. Metz, "Messianic or Bourgeois Religion?" 15.

47. Ibid., 4.

48. Paul Elie, "The Patron Saint of Paradox," *The New York Times Magazine*, November 8, 1998, http://www.nytimes.com/1998/11/08/magazine/the-patron-saint-of-paradox.html.

49. Pope Francis, *The Church of Mercy: A Vision of the Church* (Chicago, IL: Loyola Press, 2014), 26.

50. Ibid, 57.

51. Ibid, 49.

52. George Yancy, "Dear White America," *The New York Times*, December 24, 2015, http://opinionator.blogs.nytimes.com/2015/12/24/dear-white-america/?_r=0.

53. Jack Downey, "Tiny Drops: Henri de Lubac, S.J., Dorothy Day, and Anti-Triumphalism as Radical Praxis," *Union Seminary Quarterly Review* 64, nos. 2–3 (2013): 43, see http://usqr.utsnyc.edu/issue/vol-64-23/.

54. Metz, "Messianic or Bourgeois Religion?" 11.

9

Resurrection as Dangerous Memory

Mercy, Freedom, and Composition of Place in Levertov and Metz

Kevin F. Burke, SJ

> *He himself must be*
> *the key, now, to the next door,*
> *the next terrors of freedom and joy.*
>
> —Denise Levertov, "St. Peter and the Angel"[1]

THE GOSPEL OF DANGER

Not without reason, but perhaps too often without adequate reflection, we dress resurrection in Easter lilies and alleluias, in sunrise hues set to optimistic hymns of victory, in bunnies, bonnets, and colored eggs. But we forget about the road that led there. We race from guilt to mercy without taking the long walk to Emmaus. Anxious to get to the "happy ending," we move too quickly from the parched cry of crucified abandonment to the helpless moan provoked by an open grave, and from there to the outcries of Magdalene in the garden or Thomas in the upper room. As the poet Denise Levertov puts it, we wish to awaken in quietude without remembrance of agony,

> we who in shamefaced private hope
> had looked to be plucked from fire and given
> a bliss we deserved for having imagined it.[2]

In his political theology, Johann Baptist Metz guards against the false hope of an Easter without danger. Thus, he draws attention to the experience of Holy Saturday to safeguard Christian faith from abstract, idealized conceptions of resurrection. "In Christology we have lost the way between Good Friday and Easter Sunday. We have too much pure Easter Sunday Christology….The story of a journey is integral to Christology. What is called for is the experience of Holy Saturday and precisely the kind of Holy Saturday language in our Christology which is not, as in mythology, simply the language of the victor."[3] For Metz, nothing disfigures the Christian gospel quite like a proclamation of resurrection abstracted from the history of suffering and injustice, of crucifiers and crucifixions. "There is no understanding of the resurrection that would not have to be developed passing through the memory of suffering. There is no way of understanding the glory of the resurrection that would be free of the darkness and threats found in humanity's history of suffering. A *memoria resurrectionis* which was not understood as a *memoria passionis* would be sheer mythology."[4]

Resurrection as a historyless answer to all suffering and loss becomes severed from prophecy, hope, and mercy. Even worse, this abstraction disfigures other core themes in Christology: incarnation, salvation, discipleship, and second coming. To counter the threat posed by abstract and idealized approaches to Christian theology, Metz developed what he calls "a political theology of the subject."[5] He does not rely on an older metaphysical framework or the idealistic epistemologies utilized by many mid-twentieth-century theologies. Instead, he turns to categories drawn from the biblical tradition—memory, narrative, lamentation, celebration, solidarity, and the like—to address the challenges of living genuine religious faith and hope in the aftermath of world wars, cold wars, and wars of terror; of grossly uneven and unfair globalization; of the potentially dehumanizing effects of new sciences and information technologies; of a growing uneasiness with this multicultural, multireligious, postmodern world; of our intensifying awareness of the cost of this new age in human suffering and planetary endangerment.

One of Metz's penetrating theological innovations entails his use of *dangerous memory* as a crucial resource for saving the human subject. Dangerous memories are dangerous because they locate humans in the concrete histories of suffering. Thus, as a German Christian growing up during the rise of Nazism, Metz found himself particularly compelled to confront "that public history that bears so catastrophic a name as Auschwitz."[6] So too, following his intuition, we begin to read about other historical cataclysms—the Middle Passage and Wounded Knee, the Gulag Archipelago and the Cultural Revolution, El Mozote and Abu Ghraib—as dangerous memories. In each case, Metz urges the Christian churches to confront unthinkable historical suffering and offer "a witness of truth in history: 'The Word became flesh.'"[7] Such historical witness is demanded especially of the theologian because "historical situations are inherent in the logos of theology."[8]

This historical concreteness is crucial for Christology, where the Logos does not bypass history but impels the disciple of Jesus to face history. Metz recalls a saying attributed to Jesus that does not appear in the New Testament but in the writings of the early church father Origen: *Whoever is close to me, is close to the fire; whoever is far from me, is far from the kingdom.* After quoting this saying, Metz comments, "It is dangerous to be close to Jesus, it threatens to set us afire, to consume us."[9] It is not difficult, perhaps, to see how this danger applies to the life and death of Jesus, to the Pentecost-fueled missions of the first apostles, or to various accounts of Christian martyrdom. But the formula Metz uses to identify the quintessential dangerous memory of Christian identity does not stop with the passion and death of Jesus. Over and over, Metz points to the *memoria passionis, mortis, et resurrectionis Jesu Christi.*[10] Here, suddenly, a perplexity appears. Does danger also lurk in the remembrance of resurrection? In what might that danger consist? What does resurrection threaten and who is endangered by it?

An avenue for exploring this perplexity opens in a surprising place: the religious poetry and Holy Saturday journey of one of the great political poets of our age, Denise Levertov (1923–1997). In this essay, utilizing critical categories drawn from Metz's political theology to frame my reading of resurrection and its endangering effects—the disruption of social roles, the consequences of mercy, and a freedom grounded in the history of suffering—I sketch Levertov's life, conversion, and poetic explorations of resurrection. I probe how dangerous memories of faith encountering history, woven through her Holy Saturday journey, gave voice to a new poetic narration and practice of resurrection faith.

A POET IN THE WORLD

Denise Levertov was born and raised near London and educated entirely at home. Her mother, Beatrice Spooner-Jones, grew up in Wales, the descendent of a locally famous mystic, Angell Jones of Mold. She imparted to her daughter an abiding reverence for nature and the cadences of the rustic Welsh countryside, along with a love for poetry, art, music, and story. Denise's father was born in Russia. Paul Phillip Levertoff was a Hasidic Jew whose ancestors included the famous Rabbi Schneur Zalman. He became a Christian and eventually an Anglican priest after reading the New Testament, but as a scholar of Jewish mysticism and a pastor of a small Anglican congregation, he always thought of himself as a Jew who had found the Messiah. His gift to his daughter and his congregation:

> It was
> Hasidic lore, his heritage,
> he drew on to know
> the Holy Spirit as Shekinah.[11]

Levertov's only sister, Olga, to whom Denise dictated her first poems around age five, represented a third early influence. Inspired by Olga's communist sympathies, Denise was selling copies of *The Daily Worker* door to door when she was eleven. At sixteen, with the onset of World War II and the bombings of London, she published her first poem, "Listening to Distant Guns," even as her parents made room in their home for ten Jewish children who were refugees from Nazi Germany.

After the War, Levertov married an American writer, Mitchell Goodman. They moved to the United States where their only son was born in 1949 and Levertov began "relearning" the English language in an American idiom. Her great mentors and friends in this endeavor included poets William Carlos Williams, Robert Creeley, and Robert Duncan. She began also to fashion a new political sensibility in relation to such literary activists as Dorothy Day, Thomas Merton, Daniel Berrigan, and Muriel Rukeyser. Between 1956 and 1964 she published five books of poetry and found recognition as one of the leading American poets of a new generation. She opened her first book of critical essays, *The Poet in the World*, with a short poetic creed written in 1959: "I believe poets are instruments on which the power of poetry plays. But they are also *makers*, craftsmen: it is given to the seer to see, but it is then his responsibility to communicate what he sees, that they who cannot see may see, since we are 'members of one another.'"[12]

At the time of the Vietnam War, Levertov's husband, Mitch, was tried as one of the "Boston Five" and found guilty of conspiracy to abet acts of draft resistance.[13] Denise herself became one of the founding members of Artists and Poets Against the War, honing her craft as a political poet, and suffering the reactions of critics and even close friends. She was accused of politicizing and even prostituting her poetic gift. Her book *To Stay Alive* (1971), was especially controversial, and disagreement on the role of poetry in civil protest virtually destroyed her remarkable friendship with Robert Duncan.[14] Nevertheless she continued to publish and to protest. She traveled with a peace delegation to Hanoi and met with fellow poets in Moscow in the early 1970s. In the decade to follow, as the war in Vietnam rattled to an unseemly close, she turned her political energies toward environmental causes, antinuclear proliferation, and protests of U.S. military interference in Central America. Her passion for solidarity, peace, truth telling, and justice blossomed in a life dedicated to what William F. Lynch calls "building the human city."[15] Levertov concludes her moving poem "Beginners" with this lament:

> We have only begun to know
> the power that is in us if we would join
> our solitudes in the communion of struggle.
>
> So much is unfolding that must
> complete its gesture,
>
> so much is in bud.[16]

Poetry was Denise Levertov's vocation. She continued to refine the creed by which she lived and wrote. "I believe in inspiration, to which intelligent craft serves as midwife...and in the obligation of the artist to adhere to vision...to work from within." But her aesthetic principles merged with equally pronounced ethical themes: "I believe that artists, particularly writers, have social responsibilities."[17] By the end of her life, she had published nineteen volumes of poems,[18] along with collections of translations, letters, memoirs, and three important volumes of poetry criticism. She became one of the signal voices of twentieth-century American poetry.

THE WOMAN WHO WROTE HERSELF INTO FAITH

The long journey that brought Denise Levertov to a new country as a young wife and mother positioned her to morph into an American poet with a profound political spirituality. Yet her passion was punctuated with a kind of religious emptiness. From her earliest publications, she produced poetry shot through with biblical, sacramental, and theological images. At the same time, however, she had abandoned the formal religious practice of her earlier upbringing. Indeed, for several decades she identified herself broadly as an agnostic whose religious hungers were marked by "a regretful skepticism which sought relief in some measure of pantheism."[19]

A gifted thinker well versed in Enlightenment and post-Enlightenment reflection, Levertov began entertaining a suspicion that the turn to politics and history, like the philosophical turn to the critical reason of the subject, could beget no true hope. Her dawning realization finds rich theological correlation in Metz's reflections on the dialectics between religious redemption, enlightenment emancipation, and the history of suffering. "The autonomy and maturity of total enlightenment is full of internal contradictions. It is based on a subject of action whose identity has been suspended in part or entirely."[20] Feeling deeply the crisis of history's subject in her own suspended identity, Levertov voiced her despair over a purely rational political "answer" to the history of suffering:

> We turn to history looking
> for vicious certainties through which
> voices edged into song....

Reason has brought us
more dread than ignorance did....

O dread,
wind that sweeps up the offal of lies,
sweep my knowledge, too, into oblivion,

drop me back in the well.

No avail.[21]

Levertov did not remain at the bottom of a dry well. She did not abandon her commitment to political action or her passion for those who suffer in history. But almost without realizing it, she began also to reawaken to the possibilities of Christian hope in the practice of political solidarity and peace work. It did not happen overnight. There was no singular, startling interruption. Rather, after long, tiring bouts wrestling with spiritual questions and theological perplexities (the image of Jacob wrestling with the angel was among her favorite motifs), she gradually, almost inchoately began once again "breathing the water" of Christian faith and practice.[22] As she tells it, she virtually "wrote herself" into faith. A crucial period unfolded as she worked on a long, six-part poem that drew inspiration from the liturgical form of the Mass. In her working drafts, she called it "An Agnostic Mass." She based "each part on what seemed its primal character: the Kyrie a cry for mercy, the Gloria a praise-song, the Credo an individual assertion, and so on: each a personal, secular meditation."[23] Then she arrived at the Agnus Dei.

Given that lambs
are infant sheep, that sheep
are afraid and foolish...
what then
is this 'Lamb of God'?[24]

It took several months to finish, but looking back on the poem she eventually published as "Mass for the Day of St. Thomas Didymus," Levertov observed, "When I arrived at the Agnus Dei, I discovered myself to be in a different relationship to the material and to the liturgical form from that in which I had begun. The experience of writing the poem—that long swim through waters of unknown depth—had also been a conversion process, if you will."[25] Argument played a part in that process. Her political activism and work on behalf of justice, her association with other activists, especially people of faith, also served a crucial role. But it was the essential praxis of the poet—or rather, it was *poetry*—that led her, like a muse, to the spiritual awakening she captured shortly afterward in a poignant sigh from *Oblique Prayers*.

> An awe so quiet
> I don't know when it began.
>
> A gratitude
> had begun
> to sing in me.
>
> Was there
> some moment
> dividing
> song from no song?
>
> When does dewfall begin?
>
> When does night
> fold its arms over our hearts
> to cherish them?
>
> When is daybreak?[26]

In her return to active Christian faith, Levertov wrote numerous poems touching on important Christian images and doctrinal themes, including, among others: annunciation, ascension, the harrowing of hell, faith and doubt, mercy, revelation, salvation, incarnation, and resurrection. In what follows, I focus on resurrection. I consider three poems that track her poetic religious journey while illuminating how a political theology that regards resurrection as dangerous memory might animate Christian witness, mercy, and discipleship.

A COMPOSITION DECENTERED: THE SERVANT GIRL AT EMMAUS[27]

The Gospels model bad manners and the transgression of social norms. The primary offender, of course, is Jesus himself. Before his death, he dined with sinners and outcasts, touched lepers, and let women touch him. He brought tax collectors into his inner circle, but paid no due deference to high priests and the codes they enforced. Yet the history of Christianity could be told as an effort to whitewash this pattern of interruptive behavior by putting people back in their places, restoring order in the sanctuary, and reconstituting the social hierarchy. It is part of the brilliance of Metz that he allows the biblical text to speak its original, unsettling fire. "The shortest definition of religion: interruption."[28] This has implications for all who speak with religious authority. It demands of us "a new and elementary respect for all men and women when it comes to talking about God....God is either a theme for all humanity, or it is no theme at all!"[29]

In the dawn light that accompanied her recovery of Christian faith, Levertov began to place herself in the narratives of the New Testament. Initially this felt dangerous. She did it "with some temerity," for it "seemed at the time of writing to risk presumption."[30] But something was stirring. Her poetic intuition recognized the universal human competence for God of which Metz spoke. In one of her first poems written after the conversion experience of Agnus Dei, Levertov produced a composition of place that employed her senses of seeing and hearing, tasting and touching, to enter the resurrection experience of another.[31]

> She listens, listens, holding
> her breath. Surely that voice
> is his—the one
> who had looked at her, once, across the crowd
> as no one ever had looked?
> Had seen her? Had spoken as if to her?

The poem is ekphrastic. It meditates on a painting by the Spanish Baroque artist Diego Velasquez. The painting, in turn, stands in a long line of artistic and devotional interpretations of the postresurrection

169

narrative of the supper at Emmaus (Luke 24:13–35).[32] But Velasquez's painting also skews that line, and it is this interruptive view that Levertov especially appreciated. She "enters" the painting as the kitchen maid in the foreground who turns to see what the disciples of Jesus do not yet see.

> Those who had brought this stranger home to their table
> don't recognize yet with whom they sit.
> But she in the kitchen, absently touching
>   the winejug she's to take in,
> a young Black servant intently listening,
>
> swings round and sees
> the light around him
> and is sure.

Levertov enters the Gospel text through the painting, which means she does so through a character who isn't there! Or rather, following the intuitions of a well-established medieval devotional practice, she imagines a person who must have been there—the servant who sets the table and serves the meal—and tells that servant's story.[33] Importantly, by following Velasquez, Levertov not only enters the text through a character who isn't there, she becomes a *minor* character (a servant) who is not only minor but *marginal* (a young black woman.) The most interruptive feature: the marginal character is the center, the focus, of the painting! Jesus and the disciples who don't recognize him are off in the corner, as if in another room. The resurrection light dawns where it will: resurrection is either a theme for everyone or for no one. That light eventually dawned on an agnostic poet who, when she named her own religious experience, did so in the interruptive biblical genre of "resurrection appearance."

DOUBT ENCOUNTERS MERCY: ST. THOMAS DIDYMUS[34]

In a second poem dedicated to "doubting Thomas," but written nearly a decade after "Mass for the Day of St. Thomas Didymus," Levertov approaches the experience of resurrection through two different gospel passages contemplated imaginatively in the manner recommended by Ignatius.[35] The poem is written in the first person. Thomas is telling his (her) story. Her religious imagination fills in many of the details (as the Ignatian Exercises recommend). She begins with a story that appears in Mark 9:14–29 (and parallels), immediately following the theophany of the transfiguration. Thomas (Levertov) encounters the father of a demon-possessed boy.

> In the hot street at noon I saw him
> > > a small man
> > gray but vivid, standing forth
> > > > beyond the crowd's buzzing
> > holding in desperate grip his shaking
> > > > teethgnashing son,
>
> and thought him my brother.

The confrontation with innocent suffering serves as the initial "composition of place" in Levertov's contemplation. Thus, when Thomas finally meets the risen Jesus, she senses that the profound roots of his doubt lie in the question of innocent human suffering. She "hears" the father of the demon-possessed boy ask,

> why has this child lost his childhood in suffering
> > why is this child who will soon be a man
> tormented, torn, twisted?
> > > Why is he cruelly punished
> who has done nothing except be born?

Having assumed the identity of Thomas, Levertov resonates with the theodicy questions of the father. It is that man of sorrows whom she has Thomas call his (her) true "twin":

> The twin of my birth
> > > was not so close
> as that man I heard
> > > say what my heart
> sighed with each beat, my breath silently
> > > > cried in and out,
> > in and out.

The second half of the poem shifts to the upper room where Jesus famously encounters "doubting" Thomas (John 20:24–29). Levertov indicates the shift with a temporal marker, "after Golgotha." This marker bears striking resemblance to the way Metz situates contemporary theology: "The situation in which I am a theologian, that is, try to talk about God, is the situation *after Auschwitz*. Auschwitz signals for me a horror that is beyond all the familiar theologies, a horror that makes every situationless talk about God show up as empty and blind."[36] The place where resurrection encounters occur is precisely the place where an unfathomable experience of suffering has unfolded. Here we touch more starkly on the danger of resurrection. It only occurs *after Golgotha*.

> So it was
>   that after Golgotha
>   my spirit in secret
> lurched in the same convulsed writhings
>   that tore that child
> before he was healed.

Try as he might, Thomas cannot "leap" to faith on the testimony of the others: he needs the actual experience of the Lord's afflicted body to take in resurrection. In that visceral encounter, Levertov's Thomas is not overcome by shame but borne up by an experience of mercy, of light and heat, and a new kind of "seeing":

> But when my hand
>   led by His hand's firm clasp
> entered the unhealed wound,
>   my fingers encountering
> rib-bone and pulsing heat,
>   what I felt was not
> scalding pain, shame for my
>   obstinate need,
> but light, light streaming
>   into me, over me, filling the room
> as if I had lived till then
>   in a cold cave, and now

coming forth for the first time,
>   the knot that bound me unravelling,
> I witnessed
>   all things quicken to color, to form….

Catechetical certainty does not displace Thomas's doubt. An encounter with resurrection mercy does. His new faith is not devoid of questions. It is not "purified" of unknowing. Levertov glimpses the implication of feeling the mercy that Thomas experienced. In a late poem that alludes to this same Johannine text, she identifies herself among those who "must feel / the pulse of the wound / to believe."[37] Alive with the question of suffering, she sees with Thomas through new eyes:

> My question
>   not answered but given
>   its part
> in a vast unfolding design lit
>   by a risen sun.

The overcoming of theodicy-laced doubt in the encounter with resurrection mercy entails a further consequence. To paraphrase Metz, resurrection mercy demands "that one will not fail to give voice to others' suffering, and to lament the ways that responsibility has been shirked and solidarity evaded."[38] Metz takes this mercy, which he analyzes under the rubric of "political compassion," a step further. "It is anything but a matter of pure feelings. Rather, it points toward a comprehensive justice, but one achieved precisely by means of compassion for and with those who suffer unjustly and innocently!"[39] One who feels "the pulse of the wound" is moved to stop the bleeding. Mercy faces suffering. It takes on the question of theodicy. It interrupts doubt. So, too, for the Church *qua* field hospital, mercy is dangerous. It indicts business as usual. It unmasks a world constructed on pragmatism and hedged bets. It delegitimizes a global order that gears action not to contemplation but to probability and "the cynical adding up of infinitesimal calculations."[40] Mercy correlates with the prophetic impulse to speak the truth about wounded reality. It is the other face of a dangerous freedom.

A DANGEROUS FREEDOM:
ST. PETER AND THE ANGEL[41]

The heart of Metz's saving *danger* appears intimately in Levertov's appropriation of an oblique resurrection-genre narrative, the story of Peter's angelic rescue from prison recorded in Acts.[42] Here, the setting is not so much that of innocent, undeserved suffering, but of hopeless entrapment. However, the cynical presence of pragmatic calculation remains ever near.

> About that time King Herod laid violent hands upon some who belonged to the church. He had James, the brother of John, killed with the sword. After he saw that it pleased the Jews, he proceeded to arrest Peter also. (This was during the festival of Unleavened Bread.) When he had seized him, he put him in prison and handed him over to four squads of soldiers to guard him, intending to bring him out to the people after the Passover. (Acts 12:1–4)

It is hard to miss the link between Peter's endangered situation and the fate of Jesus that underlies the paschal faith of Christians. The overt mention of "the feastival of Unleavened Bread" and "the Passover," to say nothing of the imprisonment itself, serves to establish the lived connection between master and disciple. The key difference — that Jesus dies on the cross while Peter escapes in an angelic jailbreak of marvelously subtle description — should not obscure the more fundamental common theme: as Jesus was raised from the dead by God, so Peter's rescue from prison represents an act of God, a kind of *resurrectionem ante passionem.*[43]

> The very night before Herod was going to bring him out, Peter, bound with two chains, was sleeping between two soldiers, while guards in front of the door were keeping watch over the prison. Suddenly an angel of the Lord appeared and a light shone in the cell. He tapped Peter on the side and woke him, saying, "Get up quickly." And the chains fell off his wrists. The angel said to him, "Fasten your belt and put on your sandals." He did so. Then he said to him,

"Wrap your cloak around you and follow me." Peter went
out and followed him; he did not realize that what was happening with the angel's help was real; he thought he was
seeing a vision. (Acts 12:6–9)

The essential action in Levertov's poem, "St. Peter and the Angel,"
retells and enhances this basic narrative. Her description scales back
some of Luke's detail to highlight her own concern with the despon-
dence bordering on despair that Peter (or anyone in Peter's plight) might
be expected to feel. She augments the hopelessness of the situation by
imagining what Peter felt, smelled, saw, and heard while chained: "raw
continual pain, / smell of darkness, groans of those others / to whom he
was chained."[44] Even more important than the desolation of bondage,
her midrash on this narrative underscores the divinely initiated call to
freedom. Like the biblical author, her interest lies less with the miraculous agency of Peter's deliverance than with its dangerous implication.
For indeed, release from the danger of prison leaves him "alone and
free to resume / the ecstatic, dangerous, wearisome roads of / what he
had still to do."[45] What Metz calls a "grand exaggeration" implied in
the resurrection narratives emerges precisely from the way they engage
history. "As I see it, Christianity is not some sort of postmodern side-
show, but rather the most perilous production of world history, since
God Godself is involved in it."[46] Hence, Peter's escape from prison does
not remove fear. Metz intensifies the peril of resurrection faith with a
concrete example and a question: "What does it mean when the Jesuit
Jon Sobrino, who only by chance escaped the massacre of the Jesuits in
El Salvador, immediately afterward came to Europe and just as matter-
of-factly returned to an imperiled life with new community members?"[47]
In Levertov's telling, Peter's release from prison draws him "close to the
fire," the frightening reality of a divine drama lived in a fully human key.

> ...More frightening
> than arrest, than being chained to his warders:
> he could hear his own footsteps suddenly.
> Had the angel's feet
> made any sound? He could not recall.

This is the ultimate danger of the *memoria passionis, mortis, et
resurrectionis Jesu Christi*: we who are grasped by it at the center of

our lives and who feel its salvific magnetism experience it as a call. The resurrection demolishes the "upper room." It scatters Jesus's spirit-filled disciples like seeds presaging a bountiful harvest. But it *scatters* them. It puts them on "the ecstatic, dangerous, wearisome roads" of all they have yet to do to help realize God's dream, the reign of God. This is the heart of every resurrection narrative. The genre has little interest in miracle. It has everything to do with discipleship.

He himself must be
the key, now, to the next door,
the next terrors of freedom and joy.

RESURRECTION AS DANGEROUS MERCY

Denise Levertov never assumed the role of a Christian apologist. When she attempted some "do-it-yourself-theology,"[48] she did so precisely to gain clarity on "the battle [she] fought with life."[49] But her poetry, so attuned to the pulse of the real, drew her like a mystic into the heart of the paschal mystery. The resurrection removes barriers. It overcomes sides. "There is no longer Jew or Greek, there is no longer slave or free, there is no longer male and female; for all of you are one in Christ Jesus" (Gal 3:28). The resurrection displaces the priest and the slave. The servant girl first caught the light of Easter in Emmaus. The resurrection grace always entails a call, a vocation. It dawns like the call of Moses in the encounter with the burning bush; like the call of Samuel, Isaiah, or Jeremiah; or like the call of the disciples of Jesus, which in the Gospel of John occurs for Peter *after* the resurrection.[50] Resurrection is the Christian vocation.

Finally, resurrection discloses mercy. It universalizes mercy's demands and invites us to become mercy's servants. Mercy, the furnace, generates the endangering fire. It is the disciples of Jesus who feel the deep, enduring flame. "Were not our hearts burning within us while he was talking to us on the road, while he was opening the scriptures to us?" (Luke 24:32). Before God raises Jesus, human beings who loved him brought his body down from the cross. On this point, both Johann Baptist Metz and Denise Levertov anticipated and embodied the words of Jon Sobrino to his beloved, martyred friend, Ignacio Ella-curía: "Your life was not just service, then; it was the specific *service* of 'taking the crucified peoples down from the cross,' words very much your own, the kind of words that take not only *intelligence* to invent, but intelligence moved by *mercy*."[51]

As in Metz's political theology, Levertov's mystical-political poetry puts the emphasis in exactly the right places. She does not begin abstractly from theological concept, but concretely from narratives that tell of the experiences of the disciple. Resurrection placed her on the "ecstatic, dangerous, wearisome roads of" what *she* needed still to do, something she expressed in one of the first poems written in the light of her Agnus Dei conversion experience:

> This is what, remembering,
> I must try, telling myself again,
>
> to tell you. For that the vision
> was given me: to know and share,
>
>> passing from hand to hand, although
>> its clarity dwindles in our confusion
>
> the amulet of mercy.[52]

The amulet of mercy is this: resurrection as dangerous memory and endangering tradition. It flows from the experience of undeserved mercy. In the new life unleashed by our own resurrection encounters, we stand in the shoes of St. Paul who once wrote, "I handed on to you as of first importance what I in turn had received" (1 Cor 15:3). Like Denise Levertov, displaced and embraced, and like Johann Baptist Metz, we who experience the dangerous memory of resurrection faith receive a call to share it in freedom with others.

NOTES

1. Denise Levertov, "St. Peter and the Angel," in *Oblique Prayers* (New York: New Directions, 1984), 73.

2. Denise Levertov, "Mass for the Day of St. Thomas Didymus: Part vi, Agnus Dei," in *Candles in Babylon* (New York: New Directions, 1982), 114.

3. Johann Baptist Metz, *Hope against Hope: Johann Baptist Metz and Elie Wiesel Speak Out on the Holocaust*, interviews with Ekkehard Schuster and Reinhold Boschert-Kimmig, trans. J. Matthew Ashley (New York: Paulist Press, 1999), 45–46.

4. Johann Baptist Metz, *Faith in History and Society: Toward a Practical Fundamental Theology*, trans. J. Matthew Ashley (New York: Crossroad Publishing, 2007), 109.

5. See Metz's classic text on fundamental theology, *Faith in History and Society*, esp. ch. 4 and pt. 3, 60–84, 169–214.

6. Johann Baptist Metz, "Facing the World: A Theological and Biographical Inquiry," *Theological Studies* 75 (2014): 27.

7. Johann Baptist Metz, "Communicating a Dangerous Memory," in *Love's Strategy: The Political Theology of Johann Baptist Metz*, trans. John Downey (Harrisburg, PA: Trinity Press International, 1999), 138.

8. Ibid.

9. Johann Baptist Metz, "On the Way to a Postidealist Theology," in *A Passion for God: The Mystical-Political Dimension of Christianity*, trans. J. Matthew Ashley (Mahwah, NJ: Paulist Press, 1999), 47–48.

10. Johann Baptist Metz, "The Future in the Memory of Suffering," in *Faith in History and Society*, 107.

11. Denise Levertov, "Perhaps No Poem but All I Can Say/ And I Cannot Be Silent," in *Oblique Prayers*, 35. See also her narrative account of her father's conversion in "A Minor Role," in *Tesserae: Memories and Suppositions* (New York: New Directions, 1995), 4–11.

12. Denise Levertov, "A Testament and a Postscript, 1959–1973," in *The Poet in the World* (New York: New Directions, 1973), 3.

13. See Donna Krolik-Hollenberg, *A Poet's Revolution: The Life of Denise Levertov* (Berkeley, CA: University of California Press, 2013), 239–44. In 1968, a federal grand jury in Boston indicted five men, Rev. William Sloan Coffman, Dr. Benjamin Spock, Marcus Raskin, Michael Ferber, and Mitchell Goodman, and charged them with conspiracy. They were found guilty and sentenced to prison, but the convictions were later overturned.

14. See *The Letters of Robert Duncan and Denise Levertov*, ed. Robert Bertholf and Albert Gelpi (Stanford, CA: Stanford University Press, 2004).

15. William F. Lynch, *Images of Hope* (Baltimore: Helicon, 1965), 26–27; see also John F. Kane, *Building the Human City: William F. Lynch's Ignatian Spirituality for Public Life* (Eugene, OR: Pickwick, 2016).

16. Denise Levertov, "Beginners," in *Candles in Babylon*, 82.

17. Denise Levertov, "A Poet's View," in *New and Selected Essays* (New York: New Directions, 1992), 240.

18. See *The Collected Poems of Denise Levertov*, ed. and annot. Paul A. Lacey and Anne Dewey, with an intro. by Eavan Boland (New York: New Directions Books, 2013).

19. Levertov, "A Poet's View," 241.

20. Metz, *Faith in History and Society*, 122.

21. Denise Levertov, "Desolate Light," in *Candles in Babylon*, 77. This poem (along with her poem, "Beginners") appears in the final section of *Candles in Babylon*, which Levertov titled "Age of Terror." That section (and the book) concludes with two remarkable poems, "Mass for the Day of St. Thomas Didymus" and "The Many Mansions" (which I touch on later).

22. This image, drawn from Levertov's poem "Variation and Reflection on a Theme from Rilke," provided the title to the volume in which it appeared; Denise Levertov, *Breathing the Water* (New York: New Directions, 1987), 83.

23. Denise Levertov, "Work that Enfaiths," in *New and Selected Essays*, 250.

24. Levertov, "Mass for the Day of St. Thomas Didymus: Part vi, Agnus Dei," 114.

25. Levertov, "Work that Enfaiths," 250.

26. Denise Levertov, "That Passeth All Understanding…," in *Oblique Prayers*, 78.

27. Denise Levertov, "The Servant Girl at Emmaus (A Painting by Velasquez)," in *Breathing the Water*, 66.

28. Metz, *Faith in History and Society*, 158.

29. Johann Baptist Metz, "Karl Rahner's Struggle for the Theological Dignity of Humankind," in *A Passion for God*, 112–13.

30. Denise Levertov, "Foreword," in *The Stream and the Sapphire: Selected Poems on Religious Themes* (New York: New Directions, 1997), vii.

31. The "composition of place" in an important element in a contemplation structured on the *Spiritual Exercises* of Ignatius; see *Spiritual Exercises*, no. 47, from George E. Ganss, *The Spiritual Exercises of Saint Ignatius: A Translation and Commentary* (St. Louis: Institute of Jesuit Sources, 1992), 49.

32. It is helpful to see a reproduction of Velasquez's painting and compare it with other depictions of this scene, such as those by Dürer, Titian, Caravaggio, and Rembrandt; see Diego Velazquez, "Kitchen Maid with the Supper at Emmaus," National Gallery of Ireland website, accessed December 1, 2016, http://www.nationalgallery.ie/en/Collection/Irelands_Favourite_Painting/Vermeer_Final/Final_Velazquez.aspx.

33. This practice receives classic expression in the Ignatian *Exercises*. In the contemplation of the nativity, for example, Ignatius models how to "enter" the story: "I will make myself a poor, little, and unworthy slave, gazing at them, contemplating them, and serving them in their needs, just as if I were there." *Spiritual Exercises*, no. 114, 58.

34. Denise Levertov, "St. Thomas Didymus," in *A Door in the Hive* (New York: New Directions, 1989), 101–3.

35. It is interesting to note that several years *after* she wrote this poem, Levertov made the *Spiritual Exercises* of St. Ignatius Loyola (19th annotation) under the direction of Fr. Lee Kapfer, SJ, in Seattle, WA. I call this "interesting" because the same sensibility and use of imagination that underlies the contemplations of the Ignatian Exercises already was operative and well developed in Levertov's sensibility and imagination as a poet.

36. Johann Baptist Metz, "Theology as Theodicy?" in *A Passion for God*, 54.

37. Denise Levertov, "On Belief in the Physical Resurrection of Jesus," in *Sands of the Well*, 115.

38. Johann Baptist Metz, "Toward a Christianity of Political Compassion," in *Love That Produces Hope: The Theology of Ignacio Ellacuría*, ed. Kevin Burke and Robert Lassalle-Klein (Collegeville, MN: Liturgical Press, 2006), 251.

39. Ibid.

40. Ignacio Ellacuría, "Utopia and Propheticism from Latin America," in A *Grammar of Justice: The Legacy of Ignacio Ellacuría*, ed. J. Matthew Ashley, Kevin Burke, and Rodolfo Cardenal (Maryknoll, NY: Orbis Books, 2014), 9.

41. Levertov, "St. Peter and the Angel," 73.

42. Like many casual readers, ordained preachers and even theologians sometimes fail to recognize that the narrative found in Acts 12:1–11 belongs to the resurrection genre, a point New Testament scholarship convincingly makes; see, e.g., Luke Timothy Johnson, *The Acts of the Apostles*, Sacra Pagina Series, vol. 5, ed. Daniel J. Harrington (Collegeville, MN: Liturgical Press, 1992), 216–19.

43. "A resurrection before the passion."

44. Levertov, "St. Peter and the Angel," lines 1–3.

45. Ibid., lines 14–16.

46. Johann Baptist Metz, "A Passion for God: Religious Orders Today," in A *Passion for God*, 152, 153.

47. Ibid., 153.

48. Levertov, "Foreword," vii. Levertov's journals include numerous examples of what she calls "do-it-yourself-theology," where she speculates on such questions as "Why couldn't the incarnation have been as Woman not Man? Why was the culture of Israel chosen?" See Denise Levertov Papers, Special Collections, Stanford University Libraries, "Journal Entry, April 14, 1986, [series 3, box 9, folio 2].

49. Levertov, "St. Thomas Didymus," line 78.

50. See Exod 3:1–15; 1 Sam 3:1–18; Isa 6:1–8; Jer 1:4–10; Mark 1:16–20 (and parallels); and John 21:1–19. It is important to note that resurrection is not narrated in the biblical tradition primarily as a miracle story, an *act of power* (synoptics), or a *sign* (John), performed by Jesus. Indeed, efforts by post-Enlightenment apologists to use resurrection as a "proof" of the divinity of Jesus (and derivatively, of the authority of the church) betray the biblical witness.

51. Jon Sobrino, "Letter to Ignacio Ellacuría," in *The Principle of Mercy: Taking the Crucified People from the Cross* (Maryknoll, NY: Orbis, 1994), 188, emphasis mine; first read at Mass, November 10, 1990; originally published in *Carta a las Iglesias* 223 (1990): 13.

52. Denise Levertov, "The Many Mansions," in *Candles in Babylon*, 116.

Contributors

J. Matthew Ashley is Associate Professor of Theology at the University of Notre Dame in South Bend, Indiana. He writes on political and liberation theology, the history of Christian spirituality, and science and religion, and has translated several books or collections of essays by Johann Baptist Metz. In addition to *Interruptions: Mysticism, Politics and Theology in the Work of Johann Baptist Metz*, his most recent book is *Take Lord and Receive All My Memory: Toward an Anamnestic Mysticism*.

Kevin F. Burke, SJ, is Vice-President for Mission at Regis University in Denver, Colorado. Until recently, he was Associate Professor of Systematic Theology at the Jesuit School of Theology of Santa Clara in Berkeley, California. Author or coeditor of four books on Ignacio Ellacuría, including most recently *A Grammar of Justice: The Legacy of Ignacio Ellacuría*, he also edited *Pedro Arrupe: Essential Writings* and, with his sister, Dr. Eileen Burke-Sullivan, authored *The Ignatian Tradition*. He is presently writing a book on the theological vision of the American poet Denise Levertov.

John K. Downey is Professor Emeritus of Religious Studies at Gonzaga University in Spokane, Washington. A former Director of the Coolidge Research Colloquium, his work turns around the critical mediation of religion and society. His interests include language and method, human rights, the new political theology, and Francis of Assisi. In addition to translating several articles by Johann Baptist Metz and editing a collection of his articles, he was coeditor of *Missing God: Cultural Amnesia and Political Theology*.

Michael Kirwan, SJ, is a British Jesuit lecturing in systematic and pastoral theology at Heythrop College (University of London) where he is also director of the Heythrop Institute for Religion and Society. He is the author of *Girard and Theology* as well as *Political Theology: A New Introduction*.

Maureen O'Connell is Associate Professor of Christian Ethics and Chair of the Department of Religion and Theology at La Salle University in Philadelphia, Pennsylvania, where she teaches, writes, and speaks on racial justice, feminist ethics, and community organizing. She is a member of POWER (Philadelphians Organized to Witness, Empower, and Rebuild), an interfaith parish initiative for equity in public education, living wages, and decarceration. She is the author of *Compassion: Loving Our Neighbor in an Age of Globalization*.

Steve Ostovich is Professor and Chair of the Philosophy Department at the College of St. Scholastica in Duluth, Minnesota. His research interests include critical theory, philosophy of time and history, and German studies, as well as political theology. Among his publications are *The Courage of Faith: Some Philosophical Reflections* and, as a member of the collaborative writing group ATG 26, *Ruptures in the Everyday: Views of Modern Germany from the Ground*.

Julia D. E. Prinz, VDMF, is Lecturer in Christian Spirituality at Jesuit School of Theology of Santa Clara University in Santa Clara, California. She also serves as the Director of the Women of Wisdom and Action Initiative, which provides leadership formation and advanced theological degrees for religious women from China, India, Myanmar, and Vietnam. She is the author of *Endangering Hunger for God: Johann Baptist Metz and Dorothee Sölle at the Interface of Biblical Hermeneutics and Christian Spirituality* and is currently working on a book on the intersection of political theology and photography.

John N. Sheveland is Professor of Religious Studies at Gonzaga University in Spokane, Washington, where he teaches courses in theology, interreligious dialogue, and the religions of India. He directs Gonzaga's program *Being Religious Interreligiously*. His publications have appeared in several journals and edited volumes, and he is a board member of the Society of Buddhist-Christian Studies.

Contributors

Johann M. Vento is Professor of Religious Studies and Theology at Georgian Court University in Lakewood, New Jersey. Her research interests include political theology, praxis theory and spiritual formation, violence and trauma, and interreligious dialogue. Her articles have appeared in several journals and collections. Her current project is establishing a graduate program in Mercy Spirituality.